COLORS OF WES ANDERSON

Hannah Strong

COLORS OF WES ANDERSON
THE FILMS IN PALETTES

CONTENTS

8	A Short Biography
16	Timeline
18	Color in Film
26	**BOTTLE ROCKET**
34	**RUSHMORE**
44	ANDERSON'S ANIMAL KINGDOM
48	**THE ROYAL TENENBAUMS**
58	**THE LIFE AQUATIC WITH STEVE ZISSOU**
66	COLOR SPEAKS
70	**THE DARJEELING LIMITED**
78	**HOTEL CHEVALIER**
82	**FANTASTIC MR. FOX**
90	ANDERSON ADVERTS
94	**MOONRISE KINGDOM**
104	**THE GRAND BUDAPEST HOTEL**
112	WES WIDE WORLD
116	**ISLE OF DOGS**
124	**THE FRENCH DISPATCH**
132	**"ALINE" MUSIC VIDEO**
136	WES AND YELLOW
140	**ASTEROID CITY**
150	**THE WONDERFUL STORY OF HENRY SUGAR**
158	**THE SWAN**
162	**THE RAT CATCHER**
166	**POISON**
170	Index
174	Acknowledgments
175	About the Author

A SHORT BIOGRAPHY

It began in Houston, Texas, on 1 May 1969—a beautiful spring morning with bright sunshine and highs of 80°F. Wesley Wales Anderson was born to Texas, an archaeologist with a PhD in anthropology, and Melver Anderson, a writer who ran his own advertising and public relations company. The middle of three sons, Wesley came after Mel and before Eric. His father was half-Swedish, half-Norwegian, and let the kids help steer his Volvo when they were out driving; his mother took the boys on archaeological digs. As a child, Anderson was shy and insular, interested in Roald Dahl—*Fantastic Mr Fox* being the first book he remembers owning—and *Star Wars*; at seven years old, he delivered a compelling (but unsuccessful) presentation to his parents on why he should be allowed to go and live in Paris. The divorce of his parents when Anderson was eight years old was difficult; he and his brothers lived with their mother but saw their father often. In fact, it was Melver Anderson who gifted Wes his first camera: a Yashica Super 8. Before that, he used his father's Super 8 to shoot a series of silent films inspired by Alfred Hitchcock. Assisted by his brother Eric, he also recruited neighborhood kids to star.

His own high school, St. John's School, would feature many years later as the fictional Rushmore Academy in his second film, *Rushmore*, but before his professional career as a filmmaker began, Anderson traded Houston for Austin, attending the University of Texas as a philosophy major and working part-time as a projectionist at the campus' Hogg Memorial Auditorium. It was in a college playwriting class that he met English major Owen Wilson, and the two became firm friends after Anderson cast him in a play he had written (Wilson was not considering acting at the time). The pair became roommates and, after graduation, moved to Dallas, where they shared an apartment with Owen's older and younger brothers, Andrew and Luke.

Wes and Owen set to work writing the script for their first film, *Bottle Rocket*, in 1992. With a volunteer crew and borrowed equipment, they shot as much of the script as they could afford (about 13 minutes) and submitted the footage as a short film to the Sundance Film Festival. Although there was no way of anticipating as much back in 1993, this was the beginning of an incredible journey—one that initially brought Wes and Owen to the attention of legendary writer, director and producer James L. Brooks. Recognizing the potential in their tiny sliver of *Bottle Rocket*, Brooks advocated for the duo, helping them to find the funding to make a full version of the film and providing some much-needed mentorship. Unfortunately, their 1996 feature flopped and made less than $1 million at the box office.

Despite this setback, Joe Roth, chairman of Disney at the time, *did* like *Bottle Rocket* and agreed to produce Anderson's second feature, *Rushmore*, via Touchstone Pictures. Having recently been introduced to 17-year-old Jason Schwartzman, Anderson immediately cast him as Max Fischer; it was the start of a lifelong friendship and collaborative partnership between them. The film also marked the beginning of Anderson's relationship with Bill Murray, who came aboard opposite Schwartzman, and would similarly go on to star in many of Anderson's future projects. Happily, *Rushmore* (1998) fared better than *Bottle Rocket*; it was modestly successful financially but critically acclaimed. It launched the career of Jason Schwartzman and helped to reinvigorate Bill Murray's career, earning him a Golden Globe nomination.

Anderson's third feature, *The Royal Tenenbaums* (2001), was a sizable step-up, featuring a larger cast and involving a New York City shoot. By this time the filmmaker had moved to New York while Wilson's acting career was taking off in Los Angeles, but the two still collaborated on the screenplay, and a rogues' gallery of stars was gathered for the cast of the family dramedy, among them Gene Hackman, Anjelica Huston, Gwyneth Paltrow, Ben Stiller and Danny Glover, as well as Owen and Luke Wilson and Bill Murray. Arguably this is the film that really announced Anderson to the world stage, winning Hackman a Golden Globe and earning Anderson and Wilson an Oscar nomination for Best Original Screenplay (which they lost to Julian Fellowes for *Gosford Park*).

The massive success of *The Royal Tenenbaums* unlocked a new level of budget for Anderson, and he began work on the *The Life Aquatic with Steve Zissou* (2004). He wrote the script with his friend and fellow filmmaker Noah Baumbach, and filming took place across Italy and aboard a decommissioned minesweeper. A shoot that was planned for three months ended up being delayed and eventually lasted five months. Although the film has found its admirers over the years, it was met with a mixed critical reaction and failed to make its $50 million budget back. *The Life Aquatic* remains Anderson's most expensive film to date.

His next feature, *The Darjeeling Limited* (2007), fared slightly better at the box office and in reviews, and marked the first writing collaboration between Anderson and Roman Coppola. The latter was introduced to Anderson via the actor and writer L. M. Kit Carson, who had been involved in *Bottle Rocket*, and had worked in the second unit on *The Life Aquatic*. Coppola cowrote *The Darjeeling Limited* with Anderson and Jason Schwartzman (who happens to be Coppola's cousin) and it was the beginning of a long creative relationship.

Anderson's 2009 stop-motion labor of love, *Fantastic Mr. Fox*, based on Roald Dahl's book of the same name, received substantial critical acclaim. The film was nominated for Best Animated Feature at the Academy Awards, but lost out to Disney's *Up*. Anderson's seventh feature, *Moonrise Kingdom*, performed well at the box office considering its relatively low $13 million budget and earned him a second Oscar nomination for Best Original Screenplay (alongside cowriter Roman Coppola), but lost out to Tarantino's *Django Unchained*.

Then came *The Grand Budapest Hotel* (2014), a dazzling dramedy set in an opulent alpine lodge, that would become a critical and commercial smash. It took $174 million at the box office and won four of its nine Academy Award nominations. To this day, it is considered one of Anderson's greatest films, and Ralph Fiennes' performance within it, a career best. It would be four years before Anderson's next film, the ambitious stop-motion adventure *Isle of Dogs* (2018), but in the interim, he welcomed a daughter with artist and author Juman Malouf.

Although it was well-received, aside from criticisms about the extent of the film's cultural appropriation, *Isle of Dogs* could not match up to the success of *The Grand Budapest Hotel*.

Another passion project followed in 2021: *The French Dispatch*, which was a tribute to Anderson's lifelong obsession with print journalism, particularly *The New Yorker* magazine. He assembled an ambitious cast of his regular collaborators and some new friends, notably Timothée Chalamet and Jeffrey Wright, and the film premiered at the Cannes Film Festival. Reviews were mostly positive, though the film's episodic structure left some underwhelmed. Shortly after, it was announced that Anderson would direct an adaptation of Roald Dahl's *The Wonderful Story of Henry Sugar* (2023), which went on to win the Academy Award (for Best Live Action Short Film) at the 2024 ceremony.

In between *The French Dispatch* and *The Wonderful Story of Henry Sugar*, Anderson released *Asteroid City* (2023), his take on a sci-fi story. It's a mixture of color and black-and-white film, with an all-star cast that includes Jason Schwartzman in the lead role of Augie Steenbeck. The reception to the film was similar to that of *The French Dispatch*—broadly positive, although a swathe of cultural critics struggled to make sense of the filmmaker's least-straightforward narrative to date.

Anderson's twelfth feature film was announced just as *Asteroid City* premiered, another writing collaboration with Roman Coppola. Entitled *The Phoenician Scheme*, the crime caper centers on the enterprising businessman/international criminal Zsa-zsa Korda (Benicio del Toro) who embarks on a perilous voyage with his estranged daughter Liesel (Mia Threapleton) and his bumbling assistant/tutor Bjorn Lund (Michael Cera) to secure funding for his latest venture.

In the thirty years since he made the first, short version of *Bottle Rocket*, Anderson's distinctive visual style has become instantly recognizable, and the subject of countless parodies, publications, and even TikTok trends. One of American independent cinema's most beloved auteurs, his love of symmetry, saturated colors, peculiar dialogue rhythms, and period kitsch have made his films distinct and easily identifiable.

For those who operate on Anderson's frequency, his work continues to delight, inspiring disciples and imitators the world over. Now more than a filmmaker, he is a brand, with merch collaborations, exhibitions, advertisements, and even books, such as the one you are currently holding, all celebrating his unique place in the cinematic canon. Aptly, a quote from *Fantastic Mr. Fox* seems to apply to Anderson as much as his animal protagonist: "We're all different. Especially him. But there's something kind of fantastic about that, isn't there?"

A Short Biography

TIMELINE

● 1 MAY 1969

Wesley Wales Anderson is born in Houston, Texas. He is the middle of three sons.

1987

Graduates from St. John's School, Houston, which would later be a prominent filming location for *Rushmore*, and begins studying philosophy at the University of Texas in Austin.

1989

Meets collaborator Owen Wilson.

1991

Graduates from the University of Texas with a Bachelor of Arts and moves into an apartment in Dallas with Owen Wilson.

1996

Makes his first feature-length film, *Bottle Rocket*, based on a short he made with Owen and Luke Wilson.

1998

His second film, *Rushmore*, is released. Anderson moves to New York City.

2001

Wes Anderson's third film, *The Royal Tenenbaums*, is released.

2002

Anderson is nominated for his first Oscar, for Best Original Screenplay, for *The Royal Tenenbaums*. He loses to Julian Fellowes for *Gosford Park*.

2004

The Life Aquatic with Steve Zissou is released.

2005
Anderson moves to Paris; he shares an apartment with Jason Schwartzman for a short while.

2007
The Darjeeling Limited and *Hotel Chevalier* are released.

2009
Fantastic Mr. Fox is released.

2012
Moonrise Kingdom is released.

2014
The Grand Budapest Hotel premieres at the Berlin Film Festival and becomes his most successful film to date.

2015
The Grand Budapest Hotel is nominated for nine Oscars. It wins four: Score, Production Design, Costume Design, Make-up, and Hairstyling. He also designs a café for Prada in Milan: Bar Luce.

2016
Anderson's daughter with Juman Malouf is born.

2018
Isle of Dogs is released.

2021
The French Dispatch is released. A tie-in exhibition is held in Bordeaux, London, and New York City. Anderson also designs the interior of a train carriage for the luxury travel chain Belmont.

2023
Asteroid City is released.

2023
The Wonderful Story of Henry Sugar is released.

2024
"Three More" Roald Dahl shorts are released: *The Swan*, *The Rat Catcher*, and *Poison*. Anderson wins his first Oscar, Best Live Action Short Film, for *The Wonderful Story of Henry Sugar*.

2025
The first major museum retrospective of Anderson's work is held at the Cinémathèque Française in Paris. His twelfth feature film, *The Phoenician Scheme*, is released.

COLOR IN FILM

Nowadays, it is easy to take for granted that films, by and large, are shot and seen in color—to the extent that a modern film shooting in black and white is a deliberate design choice rather than necessitated by technology. Of course, this was not always so. While cinema as a medium roughly dates back to the late nineteenth century, the process of bringing color to the masses was not developed until the turn of the twentieth century, with various companies around the world competing to be the first—and later, the best—at translating the color we see all around us into something on a screen. While Georges Méliès' 1902 short film *A Trip to the Moon* was the first to use color (through hand-colorization), it was not until 1929 that a feature film was produced in full color with recorded sound: *On with the Show!* from Warner Bros. Unfortunately, although black-and-white versions of the film still exist, only one of the three color reels has survived. A little better known is the first animated film made in color with sound: Disney's *Snow White and the Seven Dwarves* (1937).

But why does color in film matter? Why were so many scientists and artists dedicated to the process of bringing audiences a little closer to the real world? And why has our fascination with the colors of our favorite films endured? It is as my friend and colleague Charles Bramesco, author of *Colors of Film*, says in his introduction to that very book: "A fickle, indefinite thing, color, and yet a crucial one."

The use of color in film provides us with information that the dialogue does not or cannot. It is an expression of artistry used to communicate silently with the audience, a covenant between director and viewer. A splash of neon can indicate a futuristic setting; sepia lets the audience know that the film is set in the past. Within the Star Wars franchise, red became synonymous with the "dark side" and all things evil, while blue was the color of rebellion, and a symbol of good. This even carried through into the sequels made almost forty years after the original, proving the strength in color association among filmmakers and audiences.

Much of the meaning of color comes from centuries of superstition, psychology, and cultural studies. Soft pastels are soothing, associated with innocence and youthfulness. Rich, dark shades (ruby, emerald, sapphire) might indicate opulence, mystery, and extravagance. But cultural associations with color can also develop through cinema—consider the impact of *The Wizard of Oz* (1939), in which the Wicked Witch of the West was given green skin in order to amp up the color contrast and really show off the marvel of Technicolor to audiences. Nearly a century later, the strong association between green and witchcraft remains, with Glinda's glittery pastel pink a sign of all things pure and good in the Land of Oz.

Yet our reaction to color is also deeply personal. We all have preferences for certain colors, which shift over our lifetime and may sway how we interpret or react to a film. The global nature of cinema means that the secret messages that can exist within the color palettes of films are always open to interpretation. Consider the color white, which in the Western world (heavily influenced by Christianity) is associated with purity and innocence. In East Asia, white is the traditional color of mourning. These cultural differences, in turn, impact how we read a film with our eyes.

And over time, like our eyes, films—at least those shot on celluloid—will warp and change. The dyes in older films can fade, leaving them with a yellow or pink hue. Although it was not how the director intended the film to be seen, this still impacts our understanding of it. Likewise, the restoration process of a film years after the fact can change its color, sometimes to the chagrin of fans. In 2023, the Criterion Collection issued a box set of Wong Kar-Wai's films, with the restorations overseen by the director, in which he made substantial changes to the color grading, claiming they were in line with his original vision. Many fans disagreed, noting that *In The Mood For Love* (2000) was much greener now, and they preferred the original version. The fallout from this situation proves the emotional reaction that color can elicit from viewers.

 Color can even become a signature across an entire body of work. As Wes Anderson is known for his fondness for yellow, people might associate Wong Kar-Wai with a shade of green that reflects soul sickness, or Dario Argento with the bright scarlet of fake blood. The repeated use of certain colors creates an association within our heads, to the extent that it can be jarring (but equally exciting) when a filmmaker moves away from the colors that we have come to identify with them. When Sofia Coppola released *The Bling Ring* in 2013, many critics and fans were surprised by the film's "ugliness"—an intentional representation of the source material and time period by Coppola and her team.

 Considering that philosophy on colors dates back to Aristotle's writing in ancient Greece, it is no surprise that the topic influences much of our daily lives, even now. The way we have been educated and socialized teaches us to associate colors with certain emotions or scenarios—red serving as a warning holds true both on and off the screen, but its origins signalling danger are more scientific, as both the color of blood and the color that stands out most on a green background.

 But there is not an exact science to colors. Blue is considered a "friendly" colur, but too much of it is cold and uninviting. Red may be the color of danger, but it is also the color of love. With warring interpretations at play, it is up to us to determine the true meaning of colors, which can make things interesting in the film world. What might be interpreted as a tranquil shade of green by one audience member might be seen as nauseating by another.

In the modern age, the prevalence and ease of color filmmaking has been a blessing for audiences, but has also led to a potential lack of ambition in mainstream filmmaking. The advent of streaming means that consumers are hungrier than ever before for new television shows and films. The demand has left us spoilt for choice, but at the cost of quality. Anyone familiar with the big streaming services will probably have noticed that media made for consumption at home can often feel disconcertingly similar—particularly visually. Squeezed budgets and time constraints (plus a sense of art made by committee rather than a filmmaker with a vision) have led to a landscape in which color seems to be an afterthought, with poorly lit sets and oversaturated scenes to disguise a lack of precision in the color design.

This makes a filmmaker like Wes Anderson—so careful and considered in his use of color—something of a dying breed. In the modern age, it feels as if filmmakers are less and less empowered to develop their own visual identity and language, and are instead expected to color within the lines of a studio's vision. Even the reluctance by many studios to support shooting on film (which has a unique color and texture) sounds alarm bells.

So, perhaps there is no better time to delve into the palettes of an exacting filmmaker and discover how color has become essential to his work. In a career spanning three decades so far, Anderson has become a true visionary, to the extent that his wide, symmetrical shots and delicate chocolate-box pastels have been imitated the world over. But there is much more to his fabulous worlds than lavish production design and starry casts; inside the Anderson oeuvre exist the very joy and heartache of life itself. From glorious color to somber black and white, he is a filmmaker continually expanding the idea of what a Wes Anderson film looks like. If the viewer were to take a magnifying glass to any element of his films, they would discover the exquisite details hidden behind picture frames or within the depths of coat pockets. It is time to take a peek behind the magician's curtain.

FILMS

HARD TIME

BOTTLE ROCKET
1996

Wes Anderson and his University of Texas classmate Owen Wilson initially wrote *Bottle Rocket*—the film that would become their first collaboration—in 1992. A 13-minute, black-and-white short, it was based on their college experience of staging a break-in to try and get their landlord to fix a broken window. Starring Wilson, his younger brother Luke, and their friend Robert Musgrave, this first iteration of the film contains a simplified version of events, in which the central trio plan a bookstore heist. When the short screened at the Sundance Film Festival one year later, it caught the attention of legendary producer James L. Brooks, who would help them secure the funding to expand it into a feature debut. Three years after that, *Bottle Rocket* (the feature film) was released, quietly announcing the arrival of the Wilson brothers, and—of course—Wes Anderson the filmmaker.

Expanded into a feature film, *Bottle Rocket* focuses on the relationship between best friends and petty criminals Anthony Adams (Luke Wilson) and Dignan (Owen Wilson) as they attempt to pull off various robberies. As the action unfolds, Anthony meets, and falls in love with, a hotel maid named Inez, much to Dignan's dismay. The offbeat crime caper was not an instant success (in fact, the feature was rejected from the Sundance Film Festival), but has become beloved in the years since.

The biggest change made between the short and feature versions of *Bottle Rocket* (beyond the length) is the use of color. *Bottle Rocket*'s first iteration seems inspired by the black-and-white, conversation-heavy films of Woody Allen, or perhaps even Jim Jarmusch's *Stranger Than Paradise* (1984) and *Down By Law* (1986). The film's fast-paced, pop-culture-heavy dialogue also evokes the work of Quentin Tarantino, whose *Reservoir Dogs* was the indie cinema breakout of 1992. It is a very solid short film, with moody, black-and-white 16mm and an awful lot of action packed into less than a quarter of an hour. Various shots and scenes would be reused within the feature film.

For the 91-minute version of *Bottle Rocket*, Anderson and his cinematographer Robert Yeoman (who has shot all of Anderson's live-action films to date) opted to swap to color (and 35mm), capturing the bold, sunny atmosphere of Anderson and the Wilson brothers' native Texas in all its glory. Here, we start to see the style that later became so easily identifiable as "Wes Anderson" begin to take shape, through carefully composed wide shots, bright, memorable costumes, and architecturally interesting locations [OPPOSITE].

#F8E073
R248 G224 B115

#82927E
R130 G146 B126

#C03436
R192 G52 B54

#ECD5BA
R236 G213 B186

Although *Bottle Rocket* was Anderson's first feature film, and therefore limited in budget, his ambition was certainly not restrained. When we are first introduced to Anthony, he is preparing to leave a voluntary psychiatric unit, sporting the red zip-up sweater that becomes his most memorable outfit in the film [PAGES 28–29, TOP]. The color red is naturally associated with both love and danger (two things Anthony is not short on). The same shade repeats later, in the motel where Anthony, Dignan, and Bob "lay low," and later still in Anthony's valet uniform, in Mr. Henry's couch, and in the Volkswagen van the gang uses as a getaway vehicle in their grand heist [PAGES 32–33]. The bold shade stands out against the bright-blue Texan sky, but also provides a simultaneous contrast and complement to the yellow that Dignan favors.

This is the yellow of his blond buzzcut, the sparks from the fireworks he buys [PAGES 28–29, BOTTOM], and of the jumpsuit he proudly wears as a tribute to his idol, Mr. Henry [TOP]. The color is associated with youth and innocence, both of which Dignan possesses, despite being unable to stay on the right side of the law. The color would become a frequent fixture in Wes Anderson's filmography, but it all begins with Dignan, guileless and hare-brained as he is.

Where the Texas of Anderson's sophomore feature *Rushmore* is often cool and muted, the Texas of *Bottle Rocket* is bright and light, emphasizing near-cloudless blue skies and swimming pools [BOTTOM], and lingering on lush, open spaces, from green fields to large suburban houses with plenty of natural light. The richness of the colors in *Bottle Rocket* provides buoyancy that balances the sometimes dark content of the story— these are criminals after all, even if depicted in a decidedly zany fashion. Moreover, this is a romantic's view of Texas, seen by someone with great affection for it. Perhaps this is why *Bottle Rocket* needed to be shot in color when Anderson realized it as a feature film. The broody black and white might be perfect for Jean-Luc Godard's *Breathless* (1960; a favorite of Anderson's and an ostensible influence on the romance between Anthony and Inez), but in the madcap world of Anthony and Dignan, pops of primary color and densely saturated film stock help bring to life a world of reckless schemes and 75-year plans, where the biggest lesson our cast of characters has to learn is about the painful reality of growing up.

● #BEB4AA R190 G180 B170

● #754E29 R117 G78 B41

● #C89C46 R200 G156 B70

● #5F3C28 R95 G60 B40

● #733728 R115 G55 B40

● #86C0B6 R134 G192 B182

SCHOOLBOY BLUES

RUSHMORE
1998

In contrast to the films that would come later in his career, the early works of Wes Anderson are marked by their more grounded settings and styling. Working again with cinematographer Robert Yeoman, following their successful collaboration on *Bottle Rocket*, Anderson looked to the stuffy surrounds of a Texan boarding school for his first project with Jason Schwartzman, who soon became a firm friend and creative partner. *Rushmore* is one of the filmmaker's less-seen, but no-less-beloved films, having garnered a devoted fanbase since its premiere in 1998. Later in his career, Anderson would become more readily associated with bright pastels and his fondness for the color yellow, but in *Rushmore* he opts for a muted, fall color palette—one that reflects the somber, restrictive hallways of the prestigious prep school, Rushmore Academy, and that encapsulates the loneliness and isolation of the film's central trio.

The film follows an eventful four-month period in the life of 15-year-old Max Fischer (Schwartzman), a precocious scholarship student who makes up for his lack of academic enthusiasm and social awkwardness by devoting himself to the pursuit of extracurricular activities. These include, but are not limited to, fencing (co-captain), beekeeping (president), Model United Nations (Russia), debate (captain), and Yankee Racers (founder).

After local business magnate Herman Blume (the first appearance of Anderson's "good-luck charm" Bill Murray) gives a speech at his school, Fischer develops a friendship with him, while simultaneously attempting to woo enigmatic new first-grade teacher Rosemary Cross (Olivia Williams) and avoid the wrath of Principal Nelson Guggenheim (Brian Cox), who is rapidly reaching the end of his tether with Max's eccentricities.

While the seeds of Anderson's signature style were planted in *Bottle Rocket*, they blossomed within *Rushmore*, where his fondness for symmetry, wide angles, and exquisitely rendered details set him apart from his peers in the rough-and-ready world of 1990s independent US cinema—Steven Soderbergh, Spike Jonze, and David Fincher, for example. Set predominantly during fall/winter in the middle-class suburbs of Houston, Texas, the landscape of *Rushmore* is defined by its cool tones—overcast gray skies, yellow-green expanses of grass [BOTTOM], and blue school shirts [TOP]. It does not often snow in Houston, but the weather here is still typified

● #752223
R117 G34 B35

● #9A94A2
R154 G148 B162

● #2B2F64
R43 G47 B100

● #B9A046
R190 G157 B88

● #4D5A4E
R77 G90 B78

● #F0F3F8
R240 G243 B248

by browns, greens, blues, and grays, and there is a slight transition (noticeable mostly in the rolling fog) that comes as the seasons change.

Max Fischer is set apart by his signature red beret. No other student at his school wears one, and although the hat matches the small red details on his school tie and badges, it is arguably the most noticeable costume detail in the film. It is also a color Max favors on his business card and, later, for the table decorations at the premiere of his play, suggesting it is a personal favorite. The pops of red stand out in an otherwise restrained cinematic palette. Red is defined as the color of passion—which, despite his flaws, Max has in spades, both for Rushmore and the unobtainable Miss Cross.

Red is also a color that Rosemary is drawn to, perhaps indicating her connection with Max, even if she repeatedly rebuffs his adolescent advances. From something as simple as her red pen for marking papers to her overcoat, which almost perfectly matches the shade of Max's beret, the color ties them together [PAGES 38–39]. By contrast, Herman is mostly seen in dark suits styled with a matching yellow shirt and tie [TOP]—less sartorially savvy than Max's offbeat, but snappy, wardrobe, but again connected to Rosemary, whose classroom and dining room are painted a similar light-yellow shade [BOTTOM]. Herman *does* wear red once, though—a fetching pair of Budweiser beer-branded swimming shorts, as he wanders laconically around his sons' birthday party.

#C6BC76
R198 G188 B118

#C46150
R196 G97 B80

#8C93B2
R140 G147 B178

#96231E
R150 G35 B30

#3C4724
R60 G71 B36

#C2D7A6
R194 G215 B166

Water is a recurring feature throughout *Rushmore*, first in the dirty green of Herman's swimming pool, which we see him dive into in a fugue state, reflecting his waning interest in the world around him [OPPOSITE]. He sits, throwing golf balls into the pool, while his sons squabble over their presents and his wife flirts with another man, seemingly too apathetic to intervene with either. Herman's murky swimming pool gives way to the ocean, as it is revealed that Rosemary has a passion for marine life—Max subsequently schemes to build a campus aquarium in an effort to impress her. This kernel of an idea to win her heart is planted in Max's brain during a scene in which she shows him her classroom tanks and the pair of them gaze at a small collection of brightly colored neon tetra fish [PAGES 42–43].

The world around Max seems melancholy, which reflects the sense of grief that permeates the film, despite its whimsical flourishes and upbeat soundtrack of 1960s hits. Max, Herman, and Rosemary are all grieving in different ways. For Max, it is the loss of his mother, which occurred several years before, but may account in part for his full-bodied dedication to Rushmore. For Rosemary, it is the premature death of her husband, Edward Appleby. Herman's grief is more nebulous, and might arguably be referred to as a mid-life crisis—he's grown distant from his wife and feels no connection with his two jock sons, who attend Rushmore with Max. Their loneliness brings the trio together and sets in motion the love triangle that fuels the film's action.

Ultimately, the relationship between Max and Rosemary cannot develop beyond a friendship, despite her remarking that he reminds her of her late husband. Instead, Rosemary briefly pursues a romance with Herman—when Max finds out, he is understandably furious, and red becomes the color of revenge. We spot it on Herman's wife's scarf when Max meets her to reveal the affair, and in the writing scrawled on the case of bees he unleashes in Herman's hotel room.

After his expulsion from Rushmore, following a frosty reception to his aquarium scheme, Max moves to the public Grover Cleveland High School, which initially seems to be hostile to his eccentricities. Yet Max is not bullied for his offbeat personality, in the storybook world of Wes Anderson. Instead, he and his new classmates stage his latest play, a Vietnam War epic entitled *Heaven & Hell*, which he uses as a pretence to reunite Rosemary and Herman, having had a change of heart about their relationship. Against the scenery of fake trees and camo, once again Max's red beret stands out—a small symbol of his resilience, and that despite his personal growth, his unique spirit has not been dampened.

● #69B6AE R105 G182 B174

 #2B5C7C R43 G92 B124

 #2C504D R44 G80 B77

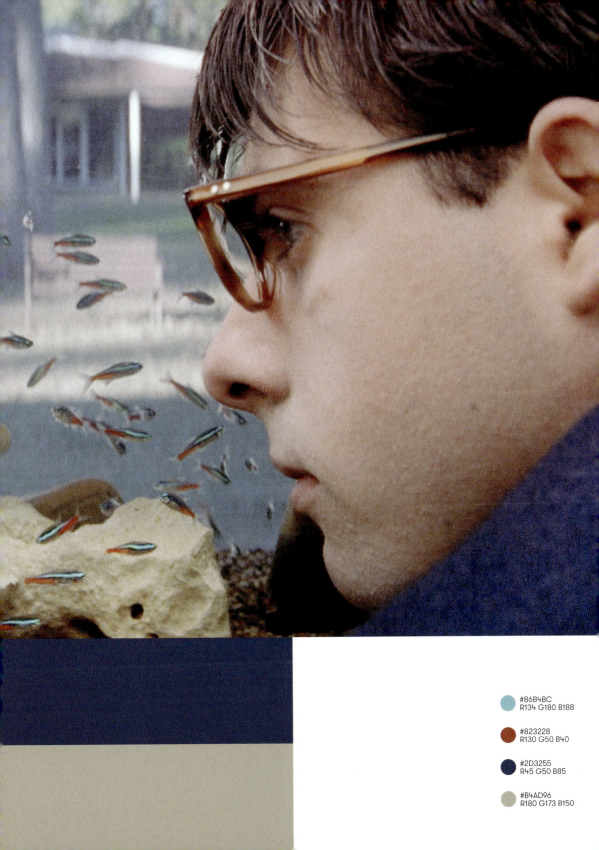

Leopard sharks, Dalmatian mice, fantastic foxes—throughout the cinema of Wes Anderson, animals play a surprisingly important role, with their unique patterns and hues adding both visual flair and narrative significance. Although this is most obvious in his two stop-motion films featuring anthropomorphic animals—*Fantastic Mr. Fox* and *Isle of Dogs*—the relationship between man and beast is strong throughout his filmography, beginning with the brightly colored neon tetra fish in Rosemary Cross' classroom tanks in *Rushmore*. Her fascination with sea life inspires Max Fischer to build a school aquarium dedicated to her, which lands him in hot water with Principal Nelson Guggenheim. Still, the oceanic blues and greens complement the film's fall color palette—a chillier one than we are used to seeing from Anderson—reflecting the isolation and melancholy of Max, Rosemary, and Herman Blume, as well as the nip in the south-east Texas air.

Oceanic life has a larger role to play in *The Life Aquatic with Steve Zissou*, Anderson's take on *Moby Dick*, in which an oceanographer swears revenge against a 10 foot "jaguar shark" that ate his best friend (Anderson delights in making up his own strange creatures as much as he does incorporating more familiar ones). When Zissou's crew members finally encounter the fearsome beast in the inky-black depths of the ocean, it is not revenge that overwhelms them, but awe. The luminescent creature—in reality, a puppet created by Henry Selick, best known for *The Nightmare Before Christmas* (1993) and *Coraline* (2009)—twirls past their submersible portholes, and Zissou decides not to blow it up to avenge his fallen crewmate. Instead, as he sits among friends, staring out at the shark, he murmurs, "I wonder if it remembers me." The shark, luminous yellow against the darkness, gracefully retreats into the depths of the ocean, no threat to Zissou and his crew.

On land, Chas Tenenbaum makes a fortune as a child, breeding whimsical black-and-white "Dalmatian mice" to sell to New York pet shops. The mice appear a couple of times in the film, and while the notion of them is inherently charming, they are just that: a charming novelty, which is how Royal Tenenbaum saw his three children. The mice—still scurrying around 111 Archer Avenue long after the siblings have left—can be seen to represent the struggle the Tenenbaum children have moving on from their difficult childhood. Later, in the film's third act, Royal Tenenbaum gifts Chas and his sons, Ari and Uzi, a Dalmatian dog as a replacement for Buckley, the beagle that is run over by Eli Cash. This could be a coincidence, of course, but that would be too convenient for a

ANDERSON'S ANIMAL KINGDOM

Team Zissou confront the jaguar shark in *The Life Aquatic*

filmmaker as meticulous as Anderson. The gift-giving—a moment of paternal connection between Royal and Chas—illustrates a recognition that the latter also needs to grow as a parent; rather than being distant like his father, he is overprotective of his sons. Sparkplug, the firehouse dog that Royal gifts to his grandsons, is not only a callback to the mice of Chas' boyhood, but an attempt at making peace.

Within the same film, there's Mordecai, the pet falcon belonging to Richie Tenenbaum, that he releases as a child after coming to believe birds should not be kept in cages. The bird returns to Richie following his suicide attempt, and Richie notes he has more white feathers. Amusingly, Richie has a similar color palette to his pet falcon—he favors tans and browns in his outfit choices. (The same could be said for his elder brother's Dalmatian mice and dog.) Their sister, ever the outsider, is represented within the film by a zebra motif, first in the distinctive wallpaper of her childhood bedroom, and then, later, in a costume she makes for a play she stages. The black-and-white stripes might have a literal connection to Chas' Dalmatian mice, but zebras are much more exotic creatures, particularly for the Upper West Side of New York City, and Margot's apparent interest in them seems to echo her feeling of being an outsider as the adopted Tenenbaum child. Even as she grows older, there are hints of her childhood affinity for the creature, in her signature striped Lacoste tennis dress and black kohl eyeliner.

Sticking with exotic animals, *The Darjeeling Limited* features two notable creatures: an Indian cobra and a Bengal tiger. The first is purchased from a street vendor by Peter Whitman, and escapes aboard his and his brothers' train, leading to them being forced to disembark. "We originally wanted to cast a little, red, spectacularly poisonous species called a krait for the snake in our story," said Anderson in a featurette at the time of filming (the krait perhaps inspired by the snake in Roald Dahl's *Poison*). "But unfortunately the only one we had actually seen had just been re-released into the wild. The most readily available snakes in Rajasthan seem to be cobras." The unassuming brown cobra is rescued by the train's stern chief steward. He claims to have killed it—but is later seen caring for the creature in his cabin, hinting at a hidden softness he would rather keep private. In contrast, there is nothing soft about the man-eating tiger stalking the jungle, which we see in a very brief scene (actually an animatronic provided by Jim Henson's Creature Shop). These two colorful creatures represent the great natural beauty that exists within India, but also that nature is not something that should be disturbed by people (a message echoed by *The Life Aquatic*).

The Whitman brothers admire a cobra for sale in *The Darjeeling Limited*

From the exotic to the domestic, dogs are by far the most prominent creatures in Anderson's films, from the wire-coat fox terrier Snoopy (tragically killed by friendly fire) in *Moonrise Kingdom* to the veritable canine paradise of *Isle of Dogs*, where each pooch has a distinctive design, from fluffy to wiry to smooth to shaggy, all rendered lovingly in puppet form. But *Fantastic Mr. Fox* proves Anderson's most fascinating animal kingdom, as much for its aesthetics as its intricate, endearing forest residents. The film's rich color palette, emphasizing warm yellows, oranges, browns, and reds, captures the cosiness of the English countryside where Roald Dahl's original novel was set. The sterile bright white of the supermarket—is in direct contrast with the natural paradise that Mr. Fox and his friends call home.

As the creatures of *Fantastic Mr. Fox* are anthropomorphic, there are similarities between them and the humans in Anderson's films. The Fox family's underground abode has in common the eclectic patterned wallpaper and multitude of clutter that make the Tenenbaums' home so inviting, reflecting the same dysfunctional, but ultimately loving, dynamic between parents and children.

Margot and Richie Tenenbaum smoke cigarettes on the roof with Mordecai, the falcon in *The Royal Tenenbaums*

FAMILY VALUES

THE ROYAL TENENBAUMS 2001

After *Rushmore* brought him some attention within the film world, Wes Anderson set his sights on a new project, with Owen Wilson as his cowriter. Considerably larger in scope and scale, it took the pair two years to perfect the screenplay. The result was nothing short of a masterpiece, earning Anderson and Wilson an Oscar nomination for Best Original Screenplay.

Focusing on the internal dramas and relationships of an affluent American family residing in a beautiful townhouse, the film drew inspiration from Orson Welles' *The Magnificent Ambersons* (1942), as well as J. D. Salinger's novel *Franny & Zooey* (1961) and Louis Malle's *The Fire Within* (1963; "I am going to kill myself tomorrow," a line spoken by Richie Tenenbaum, is taken from Malle's film). This amalgamation of references and inspirations is typical of Anderson, whose cultural-magpie tendencies are well documented (see Wes Wide World, page 112), but *The Royal Tenenbaums* is a unique film in its own right and is widely considered one of the filmmaker's best works to date.

This is one of Anderson's most striking films in its use of color. In the early scenes, where we meet Royal and Etheline Tenenbaum (played by Gene Hackman and Anjelica Huston) and their three children Chas (Ben Stiller), Margot (Gwyneth Paltrow), who is adopted, and Richie (Luke Wilson), a color palette is quickly established for each character. Chas Tenenbaum is almost always seen in a bright red Adidas tracksuit [PAGES 50–51]; Margot, in a blue, striped, Lacoste tennis dress; and Richie in a white Fila tennis get-up. Margot's and Richie's complementary outfits hint at their unique bond, and the fact that all three Tenenbaum children wear the same outfits as adults is a sign of their arrested development and inability to move on from the past. The decision to dress them all in sportswear while their parents favor more formal outfits further suggests a disconnection within the family, as does the way a young Margot and Chas look on solemnly when their younger brother—Royal's favorite child—is taken on excursions while they are left at home [OPPOSITE].

As well as being primary colors, and therefore further creating a connection between the Tenenbaum children and the glory days of their childhood, the chosen shades also seem to reflect their personalities. Chas (red) is hot-headed and obsessed with danger, carrying mostly anger toward his father Royal, while also mourning the recent death of his wife in a tragic accident. Margot (blue) is cerebral, artistic, and melancholy,

● #C26326
R194 G99 B38

● #BE4626
R190 G70 B38

● #783214
R120 G50 B20

● #73553C
R115 G85 B60

#D2B4BE
R210 G180 B190

#5A3219
R90 G50 B25

#D79B5A
R215 G155 B90

#D23020
R210 G48 B32

with a penchant for keeping secrets. She spends most of her time lounging in the bath, and disappointment is her main reaction to Royal's poor parenting. Richie (white), naive and innocent, is a peacekeeper. He was also his father's favorite—at least until his tennis career crashed and burned.

The children's bedrooms also reflect their personalities. Chas' is set up like an office. Modern and practical, it indicates his no-nonsense, entrepreneurial attitude. Margot's is a deep red, the wallpaper featuring leaping zebras. It seems to reflect her imagination but also her preternatural seriousness. While Richie's bedroom walls are teal, more emphasis is placed on his painting studio, which is a slightly lighter shade of coral-red than Margot's bedroom, and features a gallery wall of portraits he has painted of his sister. All of this information is established within the first 15 minutes of The Royal Tenenbaums, proving the importance of color within Anderson's work.

When Margot and Richie reunite as adults, they are both wearing light brown coats over their signature outfits, a brief indication not only of their connection, but of a sense of hiding the reality (that they are both still stuck where they were as children). Beyond its practicality and elegance, Margot's mink coat has become one of The Royal Tenenbaums' most enduring outfits and reflects a sense of old-world glamor about her character [TOP]. It also fits in, more widely, with the golden hues of the film, which is strikingly yellow, reflecting both the time of year (fall through to winter) and the idea that the past (that is, childhood) is not a world we can ever really return to, even if we occupy the same physical space (in this case the Tenenbaum family home).

Watching the film in sequence, most shots contain neutrals and golden tones, with occasional pops of color breaking up the scene (usually from the Tenenbaum children). There is one notable exception: the scene depicting Richie's suicide attempt. This short, devastating sequence (set to Elliott Smith's '"Needle in the Hay") takes on a blue hue [BOTTOM], which could easily be dismissed as appropriate, since Richie is in a bathroom, but knowing how meticulously Anderson plans every shot of his films, it is no coincidence. The color reflects both the peak of Richie's depression, referenced throughout the film, and his continued pain over being in love with his adopted sister; blue is, after all, Margot's color. The red blood that runs into the sink after he cuts himself with a razor blade is visually shocking in a film that is full of more whimsical touches up to this point and is, perhaps, a subconscious reminder of Chas, who lost his wife a year before. This remains one of the most heartbreaking moments in a Wes Anderson film, its impact heightened by how distinct it is from the rest of the story.

When Richie returns home after his suicide attempt, he and Margot reconcile in his childhood tent, which is bright yellow [PAGES 54–55]. Yellow has frequently been the color of optimism and safety within Anderson's work. There is something sunny and comforting about it, and in the confines of the tent, the pair discuss their feelings for one another and kiss. Despite the taboo nature of their relationship, this is a moment of happiness—one that ends the second the covenant of the yellow tent is broken.

Second only to Margot in Richie's affections is his pet falcon Mordecai, who lives on the roof of the Archer Avenue house. After being

#416E3A
R65 G110 B58

#EDAD61
R237 G173 B97

#CD5828
R205 G88 B40

#284B6E
R40 G75 B110

#6B9389
R107 G147 B137

#D7FAF5
R215 G250 B245

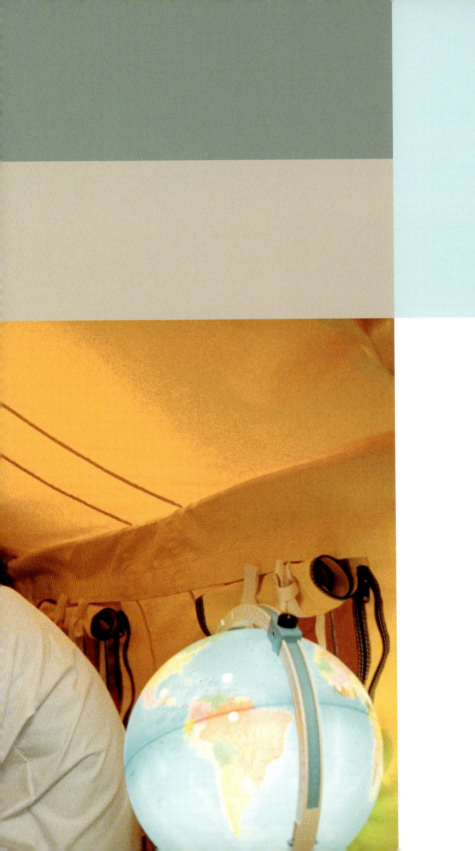

#ECB441
R236 G180 B65

#98A993
R152 G169 B147

#D8CDB4
R216 G205 B180

#D2FFF7
R210 G255 B247

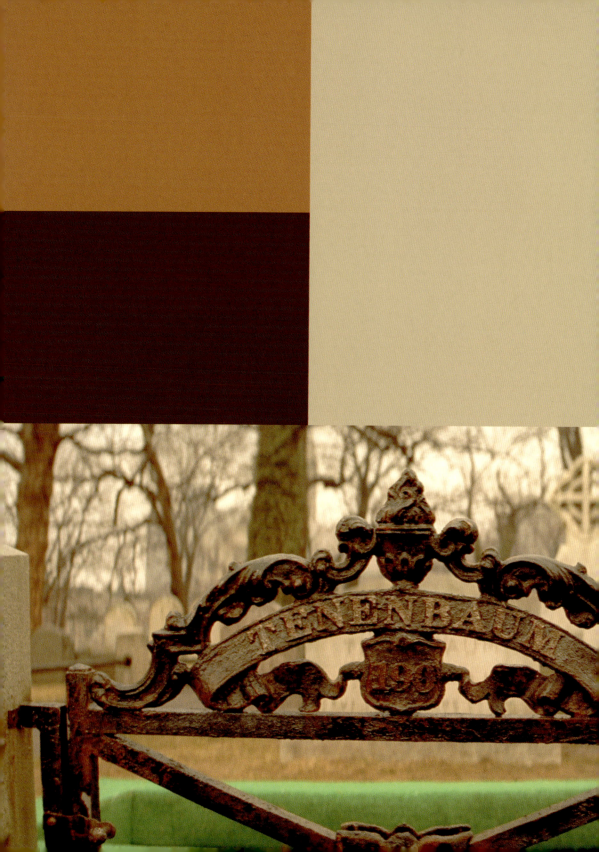

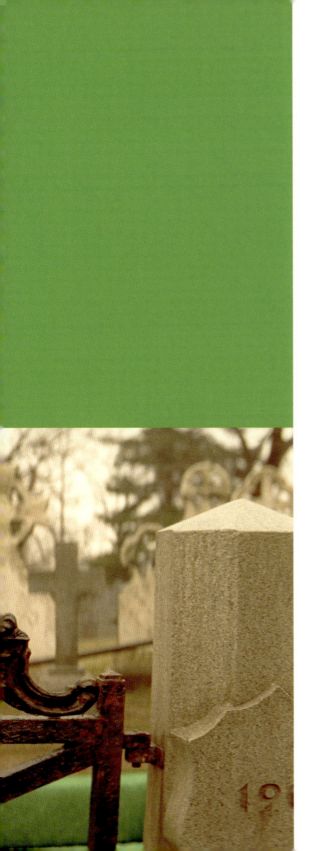

released by Richie at the start of the film, the bird returns home at its end, although Richie is not sure it is him, as he now has more white feathers. "Sometimes when people have a traumatic experience, their hair turns white," Richie remarks to Margot. There is a beat of silence, then Margot says, "Well, I'm sure he'll get over it." It's a deadpan moment of humor, considering what Richie did a few days before, but the newfound white on Mordecai's feathers also could be seen as a sign of maturing; something that all the Tenenbaums (even Royal) do as the film progresses.

In one, final, poignant use of color, there is a late reference to the Dalmatian mice that Chas bred and sold to pet shops as his first business. When his sons' dog is accidentally killed by Eli Cash, Royal gifts Chas a Dalmatian that he buys from the firemen who arrive on the scene. This symmetry is reinforced by the fact that Royal and Chas are wearing matching suits when this happens, and the reconciliation between them finally comes, as they have reached some understanding of one another. Chas and his sons subsequently wear black versions of their Adidas tracksuits to Royal's funeral as a mark of respect—when the film ends on a close-up of the Tenenbaum family plot's gate [OPPOSITE], it's a sign that Royal has finally "become" a Tenenbaum, as he always hoped to.

Although certain themes—dysfunctional families, depression, secret romances, tragic accidents involving dogs—recur in Wes Anderson's work, part of the charm of his films is how he is able to imagine such beautifully complete worlds. In *The Royal Tenenbaums* we are greeted by a lovingly realized portrait of a family in flux, and where they lack the ability to express themselves, color provides them with a voice.

● #A0732D
R160 G115 B45

● #41230A
R65 G35 B10

● #D0BC90
R208 G188 B144

● #7DA546
R125 G165 B70

SHARK TALE

THE LIFE AQUATIC WITH STEVE ZISSOU
2004

Heavily inspired by the work of French oceanographer Jacques Cousteau, *The Life Aquatic with Steve Zissou* is Wes Anderson's fourth feature-length film, following on from the acclaim he received for *Rushmore* and *The Royal Tenenbaums*. At the time, it was also Anderson's most ambitious film to date, taking place mainly on a research vessel named the *Belafonte* as a crew of documentarians and marine enthusiasts track the elusive "jaguar shark" that devoured Zissou's best friend several years prior. At the same time, Zissou (played by Bill Murray) contends with a reporter, who is on board the ship to profile him for a magazine, and the discovery that he has an adult son, Ned.

Despite lukewarm reviews from critics and a poor box-office performance, *The Life Aquatic* produced some memorable and enduring images, notably the signature red knitted hats that Team Zissou all wear, along with their special "Zissou" edition Adidas running shoes in white and blue. The red hats and blue uniforms of Team Zissou [OPPOSITE] are a direct homage to Cousteau, who often wore such a get-up, while their futuristic diving suits [PAGES 60–61, TOP] were inspired by the original *Star Trek*, as revealed in Matt Zoller Seitz's book, *The Wes Anderson Collection*. As well as being quite stylish, *The Life Aquatic* uniforms have become one of the most enduring images within Anderson's filmmaking, regardless of the film's success.

As he often does in his work, Anderson created numerous fictional creatures to populate the ocean, including the jaguar shark that Zissou is hunting, but also the rhinestone bluefin, crayon ponyfish, wild snow-mongoose, electric jellyfish, and sugar crab, recruiting legendary animator Henry Selick to create stop-motion sequences. These moments—notably the breathtaking scene in which Team Zissou finally encounter the jaguar shark [PAGES 60–61, BOTTOM]—create a sense of magic within the film, conjuring imagined life forms into existence, while also negating the need for realism. They also fit in with Zissou's eccentric persona, and the playful relationship the film has between the curated narrative of Steve Zissou and the reality.

#B4301A
R180 G48 B26

#A2B4BC
R162 G180 B188

#78462D
R120 G70 B45

#D2B491
R210 G180 B145

This is the reality that journalist Jane Winslett-Richardson (played by Cate Blanchett) seeks, tagging along on the expedition to write a piece about Zissou. Her practical khaki outfit [TOP] was inspired by British primatologist Jane Goodall (as was her name), but it also sets her apart from the cheery, bright-blue uniforms of Team Zissou.

The color blue naturally plays a big role in *The Life Aquatic*—unsurprising, given how much of the film takes place at sea, but Anderson utilizes different shades, from the playful, optimistic baby blue of the crew's outfits to the dark, somber navy in the depths of the ocean. As a color, blue has an incredible emotional range, representing tranquillity, depression, and mystery—Zissou's quest for vengeance upon the shark that ate his best friend is a direct result of the grief he has not yet processed, and reflects his own fears about the unknown aspects of the work he has dedicated himself to. But it also appears in his wife Eleanor's hair [BOTTOM], indicating their connection to one another, despite her frustration with him and Zissou's wandering eye. It is a color that binds together the characters of *The Life Aquatic*, solidifying the "found family" dynamic that appears in so many of Anderson's films.

Anderson's signature yellow also appears, notably in the color of the submersible (a literal yellow submarine) and the comically large safe where Ned's inheritance is stored, which is stolen by the Filipino pirates who invade the *Belafonte* and take the crew hostage. The pops of yellow add a degree of playfulness but also highlight the comic absurdity in certain aspects of the film—the MacGuffin of the money safe, the sofa that Alistair Hennessey brings aboard the *Belafonte* when he stops by to help out his rival, Zissou—which add some light relief amid moments of tragedy, such as the pirate attack or Ned's untimely death (another nod to Cousteau, whose pilot son Philippe died in a plane crash when he was 39 years old). It is a common misconception that Anderson's films do not deal with weighty topics. In fact, he has handled dark topics since the very beginning of his career, but he is particularly interested in how comedy and tragedy often sit so closely together in our lives, and what this means for us as people.

Two Zissou film premieres bookend *The Life Aquatic*: the first a damp squib, the second a triumph—although by the end of the film, Zissou has realized he no longer seeks the approval of his peers. Anderson is a fan of using a framing device—*The Royal Tenenbaums* is presented as a book, and he employs similar tactics for *The Grand Budapest Hotel* and *The French Dispatch*, plus the framing of a play in *Asteroid City*—and it seems likely that François Truffaut's *Day for Night* (1973) inspired the story of Steve Zissou. But even if filmmaking has a significant role in *The Life Aquatic*, it is decidedly not where Zissou's heart lies. The fact that he wears his red hat with his tuxedo at the premiere is comical but also hints at the fact that Zissou is most comfortable on the *Belafonte*, out at sea with his crew. The vibrant palette of the film reflects Zissou's love of the ocean, but also the bold personalities of his shipmates and how they come together as a family, despite their differences [PAGES 64–65].

#9BBEBE
R155 G190 B190

#780000
R120 G0 B0

#6E523A
R110 G82 B58

#A21E10
R62 G30 B16

#6B5E36
R107 G94 B54

#C4B2AF
R196 G178 B175

#A8B0AC
R168 G176 B172

#72461C
R114 G70 B28

#5A4419
R90 G68 B25

#A02812
R160 G40 B18

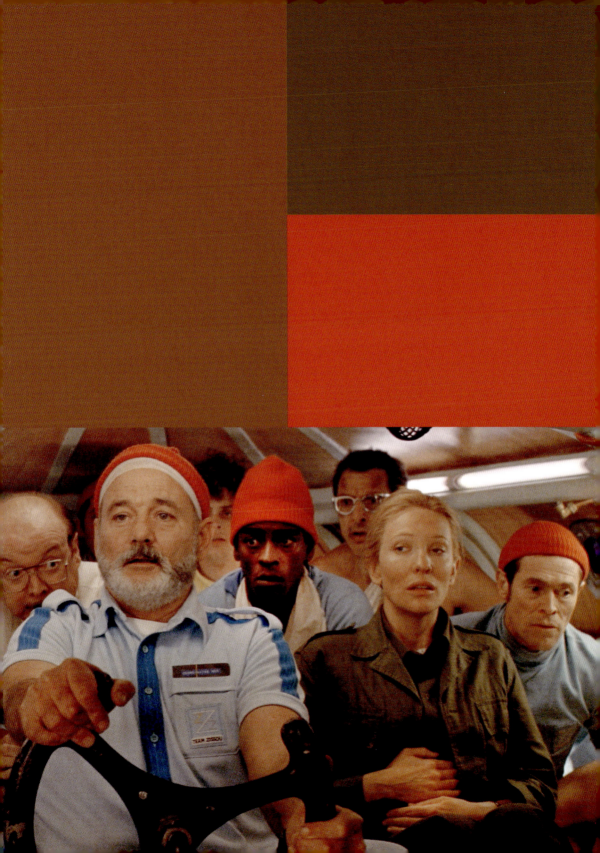

It is a commonly accepted trait of Wes Anderson's films that his characters struggle to communicate and have very particular ways of speaking. Dialogue is often stylized, not at all realistic, omitting the filler words and slang that permeate language naturally. This element of his films is among the most easily replicated; in any parody or imitation of a Wes Anderson film, monotone, often wordy dialogue will be a key feature. For Anderson, the inability to communicate properly extends beyond dialogue and is often woven into the narrative itself. What would the Tenenbaum family be without their internal fracture driven by Royal Tenenbaum's poor parenting, or the Grand Budapest Hotel without the charming, philandering Monsieur Gustave H.?

But where characters can obscure the truth or their feelings with words (or a lack of them), color within Wes Anderson's films has a habit of speaking the truth. In worlds this saturated and brightly realized, color fills the gaps in conversation; it tells us what words cannot.

While many consider *Bottle Rocket* to be an outlier in the Anderson oeuvre, due to its lack of symmetry and comparatively naturalistic style, the film certainly shows the understanding of color that Anderson has always possessed. Texas sings with primary colors: a bright-blue sky, Dignan's trusty yellow jumpsuit, Anthony's practical red sweater. The decision to dress Dignan and Anthony in these two contrasting (yet complementary) primary colors reflects their wildly different sensibilities—Dignan is idealistic and exuberant, while Anthony is passionate and romantic. Ultimately, however, these colors also pair well together, suggesting that the core relationship of the film is not the romance between Anthony and Inez, but the friendship between Dignan and Anthony.

In *Rushmore*, blue is the prominent color, indicating the isolation of the three characters at the story's heart: Max, Rosemary, and Herman. The color of heartache and loneliness, blue gives the film its melancholy glow, but also makes the second-most prominent color appear all the more noticeable: the red of Max's beret, his school tie, and his bleeding nose after Magnus punches him. It is also, of course, the color of love, reflecting the film's central conflict between the trio, as both Max and Herman pursue Rosemary romantically. It is significant that the film's most melancholy chapter coincides with fall and winter within the school year, thereby providing a sense of pathetic fallacy. Just as Max sinks into a deep depression without Rosemary and Rushmore in his life, the trees shed their leaves and the skies turn overcast and gray.

COLOR SPEAKS

A chapter heading from *Rushmore*; each segment is named for the month when it takes place (here: November), with stage curtains used to indicate Max's fascination with theater

While *The Royal Tenenbaums* is much brighter than *Rushmore*, its dominant yellow hue suggests a nostalgia that is reflected by the film's beginning, which opens like a storybook. This fairytale set-up positions the Tenenbaums within a fantastical realm. In the film, the bright colors contrast with the anger and sadness that plague the three Tenenbaum children. Whether it is the bright-red anxiety and rage of Chas in his fitting, red Adidas tracksuit or the blue of Margot that symbolizes her enduring depression, the siblings' internal anguish is reflected by their external wardrobe. Even in the scene where Richie and Margot address their feelings for each other after his suicide attempt, they are wearing their signature colors: Margot in blue, Richie in white. There is also a tendency for characters to dress in matching colors during moments of potential reconciliation—for example, Eli and Richie are both wearing brown jackets when Richie confronts Eli about his drug problem, and Royal and Chas reconcile in their wedding suits at the end of the film.

Self-expression is crucial to so many of Anderson's characters. Suzy Bishop in *Moonrise Kingdom* might wear the pretty collared dresses that her parents buy for her, but her blue eye make-up represents a small act of teenage rebellion. Mr. Fox's corduroy suit is a reminder of the life Foxy *wants* to live rather than the one he does. And while the Whitman brothers bicker over their father's belongings in *The Darjeeling Limited*, Peter's insistence on wearing items that used to belong to him indicates a desire to carry part of the past with him.

Color can be a powerful indicator for inclusion in Anderson's films, too. Think of the pastel-blue jumpsuits and red beanies of Zissou's oceanic crew, the khaki of the Khaki Scouts in *Moonrise Kingdom* or the smart purple uniforms of the Grand Budapest Hotel staff. The exacting detail of Wes Anderson's films is not just to show off, but indicates the craving for belonging that many of his characters feel, whether as part of a literal or metaphorical family. To wear the same color within a Wes Anderson film is to draw a connection between two characters—which explains Zissou's anger at Ned wearing his Team Zissou uniform after his romantic relationship with Jane is revealed.

Just as importantly, color can alert the audience to danger—in the dour black uniforms of the Zubrowkan troops in *The Grand Budapest Hotel*, for example, and the metallic silver of the robot-dogs in *Isle of Dogs*. Equally, it functions as a comical misdirection: the eerie, green glow of the alien's spaceship in *Asteroid City* might seem to indicate an imminent invasion to rival that of *Mars Attacks!* (1996), but in fact, the alien is ultimately revealed to be harmless.

Color can also serve as fodder for plain amusement. In *Fantastic Mr. Fox*, when Mr. Fox comments that his wife Felicity is "glowing," a semi-transparent, plastic model of Mrs Fox lit from within replaces the traditional puppet to illustrate the comment. This creates a visual gag for the audience, and the moment is sweetly recalled in the film's final scene, when both Mr. Fox and his wife are shown in this manner, indicating not only their happy ending, but a harmonious relationship, at last.

More somber within Anderson's films is the filmmaker's use of black and white, which began in *The Grand Budapest Hotel* and indicates more serious storytelling beats (the short film version of *Bottle Rocket* was shot in black and white to keep costs low). In *The Grand Budapest Hotel*, it is the death of Gustave H. In *The French Dispatch*, while key moments from all of the stories are shot in black and white, the most heartbreaking is the scene in which Arthur Howitzer arrives to bail Roebuck Wright out of prison. Actor Jeffrey Wright's face, shot in close-up, takes on a devastating pain, reminding the audience of the homophobia and racism of the time period, while only alluding to it in dialogue. Similarly, in *Asteroid City*, the decision to shoot the "behind-the-scenes" narrative in black and white adds an eerie gravity to it. When it is revealed that Conrad Earp died and Jones Hall is still mourning him, the lack of color adds a particular seriousness to the scene, in contrast to the peppy pastels of the fictional narrative—which is somewhat ironic, considering Augie Steenbeck is very much in mourning for his recently deceased partner, too.

There is no overarching formula for color in Anderson's films, as much as he has his favorites. But his own exacting taste extends to his characters, and color is a powerful tool for self-expression. Where characters might struggle to articulate themselves, their outfits or surroundings might provide us—and them—with some clues.

Royal and Chas Tenenbaum reconcile at the end of *The Royal Tenenbaums*

Plastic, glowing versions of Mr. and Mrs Fox in *Fantastic Mr. Fox*

INDIAN SUMMER

THE DARJEELING LIMITED
2007

Back in the summer of 2005, while Roman Coppola and Jason Schwartzman were in Paris shooting Sofia Coppola's *Marie Antoinette* (2006), Wes Anderson arrived in the city to stay in Schwartzman's guest room. He was burned out after the poor reception to *The Life Aquatic with Steve Zissou* and felt creatively stifled by New York City. After spending a significant amount of time with Roman Coppola and Schwartzman, an idea began to percolate: what if the three of them wrote a film together?

The Darjeeling Limited was born from this collaboration, after Anderson, Coppola, and Schwartzman took a month-long research trip across India by train, during which the majority of the script was written. With points of inspiration including Jean Renoir's *The River* (1951; recommended to Anderson by Martin Scorsese) and John Cassavetes' *Husbands* (1970), the trio later returned to India with Owen Wilson and Adrien Brody in tow for a four-month-long shoot. Wilson, Brody, and Schwartzman star as the estranged Whitman brothers, Francis, Peter, and Jack, who reunite a year after their father's funeral for a soul-searching trip across the country, aboard the eponymous train.

The warm palette of *The Darjeeling Limited* reflects an outsider's view of India: there is a slight golden hue to the cinematography [TOP], which is a trope commonly used by filmmakers when setting a film in Latin America, the Middle East, or south-east Asia, used to convey a certain intensity and mysticism. As the trope has become more pervasive, so has valid criticism of it as lazy shorthand.

Yet, within *The Darjeeling Limited*, color bursts forth from every frame, whether in the exquisite detailing of the titular train [PAGES 72–73, BOTTOM] and the bright staff uniforms [BOTTOM], or the rainbow of saris that we see local women wearing as they gather at a temple [PAGES 72–73, TOP]. As always, Anderson's attention to detail is second to none, although the film has been heavily criticized for appearing to appropriate Indian culture, using the country as a backdrop to the woes and squabbles of three white men, rather than affording India and the film's few Indian characters substantial depth.

This accusation is not without merit, as the Whitman brothers do cause chaos during their time as passengers on the train, accidentally releasing a poisonous snake and picking a fight with two German tourists. At several points we see a group of unnamed Indian bellhops ferrying the Whitmans' extensive luggage around. The brothers

#73280F
R115 G40 B15

#CC9200
R204 G146 B0

#DEB600
R122 G182 B0

#172E5E
R23 G46 B94

#6E733C
R110 G115 B60

#916E3A
R145 G110 B58

barely acknowledge them, and seem more preoccupied with purchasing extra-strength Indian cold medication and interesting pairs of shoes than engaging with the people around them in any meaningful way. Even Jack's brief affair with Rita, a hostess on the train, is purely physical rather than a sincere effort to form a connection with her.

But Anderson's status as an outsider undoubtedly contributes to how beautiful the film looks: it is a foreigner's view of the country, colored by a sincere love of Renoir and Satyajit Ray, but ultimately still the perspective of an affluent white American. He does seem at least partly aware of his own limitations: the contrast between the gray suits that the Whitman brothers wear throughout the film [TOP] and the vibrant world around them suggests a physical distance between the two that cannot quite be reconciled, even with the addition of *bindi* and *jaimala* [BOTTOM]. Anderson has never strived for realism in his filmmaking; the striking, stylish look of his cinema is a delicately manufactured fantasy. This is not to say that such fantastic storybook worlds cannot generate sincere emotion and thematic resonance, but it is important to remember when considering the wider cultural context of his work.

However, there is one moment of genuine connection between the Whitman brothers and Indian culture, when they witness three boys capsize on a raft travelling down a fast-flowing river. While Francis and Jack manage to rescue two of the children, Peter is unsuccessful in saving the third, and they return his body to his devastated father. In this section of the film, the mood shifts—gone are the bright colors, stripped away so that the white clothes (the traditional mourning color in India) stand out against the arid orange of the landscape. As the brothers attend the young boy's funeral, a brief match-cut flashback shows them dressed in black [PAGES 76–77, TOP], in the back of a car on the way to their father's memorial a year previously, wearing the same pensive, stunned expressions as they do in the present [PAGES 76–77, BOTTOM]. The Whitman brothers are finally forced to confront their familial fracture and pervasive grief.

The Darjeeling Limited is a strikingly beautiful film—one of Anderson's most vivid and memorable—and its flaws do not detract from this great beauty. The somber grays and dark blues of the Whitman brothers contrast richly with the lush greens and ambers of India, marking them out as stiff, uncertain foreigners while echoing the technicolor splendor of Renoir's influence.

#AC5B1F
R172 G91 B31

#3C3636
R60 G54 B54

#F0E8DE
R240 G232 B222

#E2DAC1
R226 G218 B193

#8E8C98
R142 G150 B152

#BC411D
R188 G65 B29

A ROOM WITH A VIEW

HOTEL CHEVALIER
2007

While it is commonly believed that Wes Anderson has never made a prequel or sequel to any of his films, this is not *quite* the case, as *The Darjeeling Limited* is technically a follow-up to a 13-minute short film the filmmaker shot in Paris one year prior, starring Jason Schwartzman as Jack Whitman and Natalie Portman as his flighty ex-girlfriend Rhett.

Anderson had intended *Hotel Chevalier* —which he financed himself and shot with a 13-person crew, using props from his own apartment in Paris' luxurious Hôtel Raphael —to be a standalone project. After noting similarities between the male character and one appearing in the feature-length script he was working on at the time, however, Anderson decided the short would be a sort of prologue to *The Darjeeling Limited*. Subsequently, some of the dialogue between Jack and Rhett appears in the feature film, as does the yellow bathrobe, which Jack takes from the hotel. Toward the end of the film, Portman has a small cameo, alone, in Jack's hotel room.

Hotel Chevalier is Anderson's only film that takes place in a single location: Jack's cozy, but luxurious, hotel suite, where he has been living for some time (longer than a month, he tells Rhett after prompting).

The dominant color in the room is yellow [BOTTOM], long associated with Anderson's films, and ties *Hotel Chevalier* to *The Darjeeling Limited* visually, despite being set some 4,350 miles away. But it is also a nostalgic color, warm and inviting, reflecting the sense that there is a considerable shared history between Rhett and Jack, beyond the 12-minute glimpse we get here. Complementing the yellow are the room's burgundy accents—the carpet, a matchbook, the headboard of the bed, a stray necktie, and the piping on Jack's bathrobe [TOP]—which evoke a sense of romance and passion. This provides an ironic contrast from the reality of their relationship: "If we fuck I'm gonna feel like shit in the morning," Rhett tells Jack bluntly.

Then there is the film's final scene, where Jack gives a naked Rhett his bathrobe, and they go out to the balcony so he can show her his view of Paris. It is sunset, and there is a pleasing symmetry between Rhett's bathrobe and the sparse lights in the windows of neighboring buildings, with a row of twinkling fairy lights just behind their heads [PAGES 80–81]. Even if the cool evening blues of this tableau imply the sense of an ending, the pops of yellow-gold suggest a glimmer of potential reconciliation.

#BEA88C
R190 G168 B140

#CA9831
R202 G152 B49

#BE7325
R190 G115 B37

#160502
R22 G5 B2

#442109
R68 G33 B9

#EDC549
R137 G197 B73

#A4BCDD
R164 G188 B221

#0C2448
R12 G36 B72

#CAA01C
R202 G160 B28

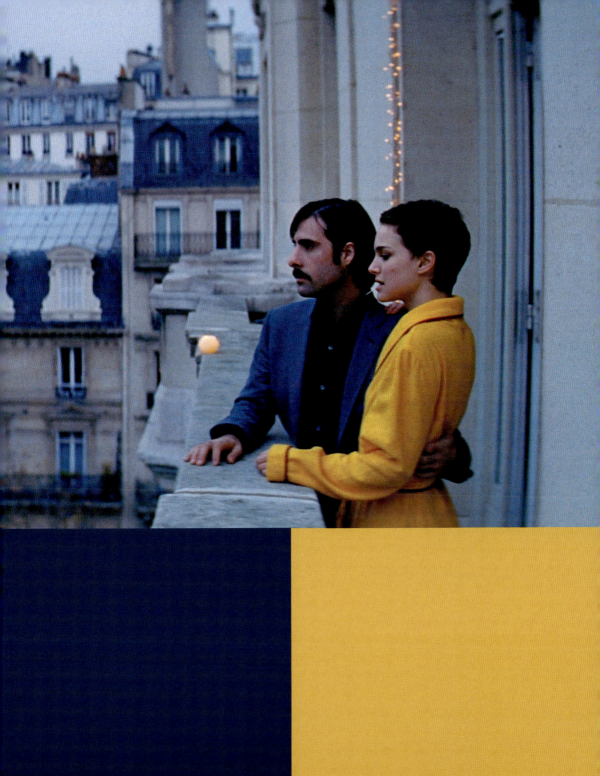

COURAGE AND CUNNING

FANTASTIC MR. FOX
2009

In a 2009 interview with online entertainment platform IGN, Wes Anderson revealed that *Fantastic Mr. Fox* was the first Roald Dahl book that he owned as a child. The story about a wily woodland creature outsmarting a group of vengeful farmers in the English countryside captured the imagination of a young Anderson—so much so, that when he began his filmmaking career, he saw the potential in adapting the book for the big screen, particularly the scenes of Fox and his friends digging a maze of tunnels. But in typical Anderson fashion—that is, favoring intricate and elaborate design—he had his heart set on a labor-intensive approach to bring Dahl's wonderful world to life: stop-motion animation. "I knew I wanted the animals to have fur—to not be Plasticine or something like that," Anderson explained to IGN. "I wanted it to be autumnal [TOP] and originally I thought I wanted there to be mud everywhere and it wouldn't be very colorful. That stayed—not the mud, but there's almost nothing blue or green in the movie."

It is true that Anderson's first feature foray into animation (having employed the technique briefly in *The Life Aquatic with Steve Zissou*) is defined by its warm color palette, rich in oranges, reds, browns, and yellows that lend *Fantastic Mr. Fox* a coziness which feels unique within the director's work [BOTTOM]. Although Anderson's love of the color yellow is well documented, his films tend to skew cooler in tone, with his sixth feature film often regarded as an outlier, at least until 2018's *Isle of Dogs*. But this film is no less immaculately staged than any of his live-action films, in no small part thanks to the collaboration of Mark Gustafson, who was brought on to oversee the animation side of the project after Henry Selick—the man behind stop-motion classics *The Nightmare Before Christmas* (1993) and *James and the Giant Peach* (1996)—departed to direct his adaptation of Neil Gaiman's *Coraline* (2009).

Together with Gustafson, and production designer Nelson Lowry, Anderson created a menagerie of distinctive anthropomorphic puppets—from the Fox family and their animal neighbors to the antagonistic human farmers, who are none too happy about the depletion of their chicken and cider stocks. Amusingly, the team found the more realistic they were able to make things, the more they liked them—which should seem strange for a film about talking animals, but in fact the life-like detail (as well as being delightful to look at) helps create a relationship between the animals and the film's audience. The red-orange fur of the Fox family blends in

#DEA25C
R222 G162 B92

#EEC88E
R238 G200 B142

#8C4B23
R140 G75 B45

#E8D2A6
R232 G210 B166

#E4C559
R228 G197 B89

#604622
R96 G70 B34

with the fall countryside [TOP], emphasizing how they fit into the natural world around them, despite Mr. Fox's initial insistence that they are *not* wild animals. Fox's obsession with stealing from the three human farmers further illustrates his longing to move up within society. Humans are at the top of the pecking order, and he sees the redistribution of their assets as a step toward achieving a more equal footing. Anderson donated fabric from his own wardrobe to create Mr. Fox's signature corduroy suit [BOTTOM LEFT], suggesting a kinship between filmmaker and subject. The rich, rustic color palette of *Fantastic Mr. Fox* also pays homage to Donald Chaffin's original illustrations for Roald Dahl's novel. Without feeling the need to adapt directly, Anderson does pull from his work, with the sartorial stylings of the woodland animals. Similarly, the earthy color palette and costuming details for both the animal and human characters suggest a late 1960s/early 1970s setting [BOTTOM RIGHT]—although there is never any defined period in which the story takes place, the Rolling Stones and Beach Boys songs used and the original publication date of Dahl's book (1970) are further clues.

While the fall colors of the animal kingdom illustrate a connection between flora and fauna, the same cannot be said for the dark and sinister barn in which cousin Kristofferson is held hostage, or the sewers the animals retreat to after the farmers wage war on them.

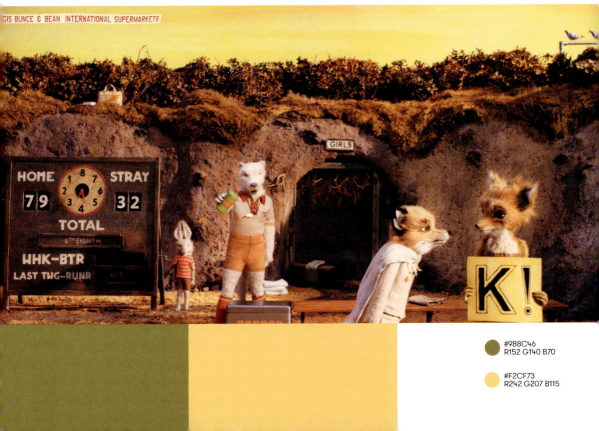

#988C46
R152 G140 B70

#F2CF73
R242 G207 B115

The local grocery store [OPPOSITE], run by the trio of farmers, is in particularly sharp contrast to the natural world, with shiny tiles and fluorescent overhead lighting—not to mention a sea of neatly organized processed foods. But this is still a Wes Anderson grocery store, after all, so the produce follows the fall color palette of the film—oranges, yellows, and reds—and there is nary a shiny apple or squab-in-a-can out of place.

One key moment of divergence from the film's color palette is when Mr. Fox and his arch nemesis Rat have a climactic showdown, and flashes of bright light alternate with darkness to create the film's biggest dramatic moment [PAGES 88–89]. The scene's dynamic use of light contrast and sound (the crackle of electricity) adds to the sense of kinetic energy the film possesses through its remarkable use of stop-motion animation, but it also adds a sense of threat to what could otherwise be a cartoonish animal fight.

The strength of *Fantastic Mr. Fox* is undoubtedly how much care and attention Anderson lavishes upon his subjects—the film is every bit as serious and involved as his live-action work, and the voice acting as sharp and emotional. Animation has long been miscategorized as suited for younger audiences, but works like those of Anderson dispel the myth that there is anything childish about the love and care that goes into crafting a film as bright and bold as this.

#A84830 R168 G72 B48
#663A4A R102 G58 B74
#C88E1E R200 G142 B30
#DCCDB8 R220 G205 B184

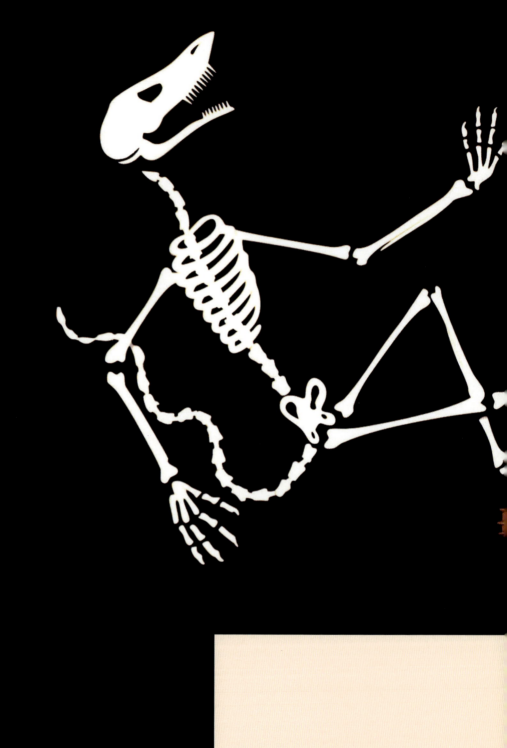

#000000
R0 G0 B0

#F6E9DC
R246 G233 B220

#AA6E2C
R170 G110 B44

After *The Royal Tenenbaums* launched Wes Anderson as a breakthrough filmmaking talent, the Swedish home-goods giant Ikea approached him to direct a pair of advertisements as part of their "Unböring" campaign. Watching the two thirty-second clips, viewers might not instantly identify Anderson as the director. The handheld camerawork, relatively muted color palette and emotionally charged dialogue seem to be the antithesis of the Anderson aesthetic. However, given that this was his first advertising project, Anderson was presumably expected to adhere to certain guidelines, and Ikea, in particular, has a strong brand identity, defined by a use of stark, neutral colors and a distinctly Scandinavian sense of humor.

The adverts—"Kitchen" and "Living Room"—each focus on a family in the middle of a tense scene. In the first, a teenage girl struggles to tell her parents that she is pregnant, and in the second, a couple fight about their marriage. But there is a twist. Each scene abruptly shifts after the bombshell moment, revealing the family to be standing in an Ikea showroom. These scenes appear more in keeping with Anderson's classic style, utilizing wide shots, clean lines, and symmetry.

Not long after the commercials for Ikea, Anderson shot a number of short advertising spots for American telecoms operator AT&T. These may lack the color that has become such a staple of Anderson's work, but they seem to have more in common with his later filmography, as the characters address the audience directly.

American Express got in on the action in 2006, commissioning an advert in which Anderson stars as himself, alongside Jason Schwartzman and Waris Ahluwalia in a homage to François Truffaut's *Day for Night* (1973). In "My Life, My Card," Anderson is on set, shooting an action movie, and speaks to the camera, while also giving direction to his cast and crew. The advert features a continuous tracking shot and is brightly lit, further referencing *Day for Night*. The quick-fire dialogue and self-deprecating humor also indicate that, even relatively close to the beginning of his career, Anderson had already developed traits that would become staples of his filmography.

In 2008, an advertisement for Japanese mobile phone provider SoftBank took inspiration from another of Anderson's favorite films: Jacques Tati's *Les Vacances de Monsieur Hulot* (1953). The short commercial sees Brad Pitt playing a hapless tourist (dressed in an outfit resembling Hulot's, in Anderson's trademark yellow) who attempts to buy some fruit, help a family with their broken-down car, and then take a photograph of a painter. With its bright colors, French pop soundtrack and zany sensibility, the short, dialogue-free spot is

ANDERSON ADVERTS

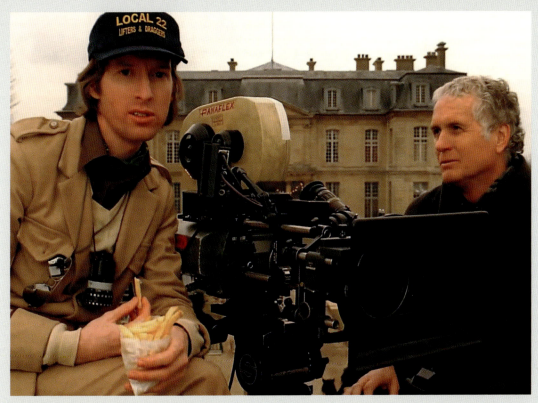

Wes Anderson in the American Express advert "My Life, My Card"

quintessential Anderson, demonstrating that, by 2008, his signature style had become a selling point in itself.

In 2010, Anderson and Roman Coppola created a one-minute advert for Belgian brewery Stella Artois, which features the fondness for mid-century-modern design Anderson is known for. "Le Apartomatic" shows a young man showing off his retro-futuristic apartment to a young woman he has brought home. Impish humor, 1960s outfits, some tech seamlessly built into otherwise classic design? This is Anderson through and through.

Differing from the many live-action adverts Anderson has created, his collaboration with Sony for their Xperia mobile phone in 2012 was an exercise in stop-motion, undoubtedly inspired by his work on *Fantastic Mr. Fox*.

Bringing it to life involved nine custom sets, 37 hand-crafted models, and more than 10,000 man-hours. The narrator of "Made of Imagination" is eight-year-old Jake Ryan (a star in *Asteroid City* some 11 years later), who explains his theory that there are "tiny, tiny little robots" inside the smartphone, who make it work. The charming advert (surprising for being handmade, given the tech-giant status of the client) received coverage in *The New Yorker*. The magazine also covered the two spots Anderson made for Japanese car manufacturer Hyundai that same year. "Modern Life" and "Talk to My Car" are more in line with his early work for Ikea, but with more of the visual affectations that have become crucial to Anderson's work—notably, a tracking shot used in the former and animation in the latter.

In 2013, Anderson worked with Italian fashion giant Prada for the first time, directing the eight-minute short film *Castello Cavalcanti* for the brand. Jason Schwartzman stars as Jed Cavalcanti, a driver who crashes in a rural Italian town square during a race, only to discover it is the home of his ancestors. The bright colors, signature yellow, tracking shots, and use of both wide angles and close-ups make Anderson's stamp on the campaign obvious. Anderson went on to collaborate with Prada again that same year, on a campaign for their fragrance Prada Candy L'Eau, creating an advert with Roman Coppola starring Léa Seydoux (who later starred in *The Grand Budapest Hotel* and *The French Dispatch*). Seydoux's heroine, Candy, finds herself caught in a love triangle with best friends Julius and Gene in an idealized, stylized vision of Paris, but has little desire to choose between them. Another Truffaut film—*Jules et Jim* (1962)—was the likely inspiration here.

In 2016, H&M hired Anderson to create a four-minute Christmas advert, for which he recruited his old friend Adrien Brody for the starring role. "Come Together: A Fashion Picture in Motion" takes place aboard a train on Christmas Eve, with Brody serving as the weary conductor, Ralph, who has to break it to his passengers that they will not be home in time for the holidays. As the camera pans across the disappointed passengers' faces within the coach, Ralph announces there will be a consolatory Christmas brunch in the cafeteria car. In the spirit of coming together, he and his crew rustle up some holiday magic for the passengers, turning the dining car into a winter wonderland replete with paper snowflakes and a Christmas tree. This is perhaps Anderson at his most whimsical and another example of how his style has become covetable to the point that even advertisements incorporating it feel like they naturally fit into his world.

Montblanc—known for their fine Swiss pens and watches—commissioned an advertising campaign from Anderson in 2024 to celebrate 100 years of the Meisterstück pen. Anderson brought in his regular collaborator Jason Schwartzman and new pal Rupert Friend, with whom he worked on *Asteroid City* and his Roald Dahl shorts. The trio provide a whistle-stop history of the Meisterstück in an Alpine cabin, as well as revealing the Schreiberling pen that Anderson himself designed. It is, perhaps, the most self-aware advertisement Anderson has made to date, with him essentially playing himself.

If his long career as a commercial artist tells us anything, it is that few filmmakers have been able to commercialize their work with as much success as Wes Anderson. While, at first, he was very much a gun for hire in the advertising world, he has now become a desirable aesthetic in his own right; brands hire him because they want to associate their products with his ineffable hipster cool. And as his profile has grown, so, too, has his creative control over the projects he takes on.

Jason Schwartzman in the *Castello Cavalcanti* advert for Prada

Adrien Brody in the H&M advert "Come Together"

GROWING PAINS

MOONRISE KINGDOM 2012

It is something of a running joke that Wes Anderson likes to tell stories about orphans—or, at the very least, children missing one parent. Max Fischer, Ari and Uzi Tenenbaum, Ned Zissou, the Whitman Brothers, Zero the Lobby Boy, Atari Kobayashi, the Steenbeck children—the list goes on. Perhaps none are as unfortunate as 12-year-old Sam Shakusky (Jared Gilman), the Khaki Scout at the center of *Moonrise Kingdom*. After losing both of his parents at a young age, he was shunted through the foster-care system and subjected to bullying, leading to "emotional issues" that left him at the mercy of social services. It is something of a miracle, then, when he meets fellow outsider Suzy Bishop (Kara Hayward) and the pair conspire to run away together. Understandably, the adults of New Penzance Island are less happy about this blossoming romance and set out to track them down.

At its heart, *Moonrise Kingdom* is a love story—the most overt that Anderson has told, although romance features in all his films. In an interview with online publication Collider at the time of the film's release, he discussed his interest in imagining a romance between children: "I remember this feeling, when I was in fifth grade [...] nothing really happened. I just experienced the period of dreaming about what might happen, when I was at that age."

Taking inspiration from François Truffaut's *The 400 Blows* (1959) and *Small Change* (1976), as well as from his youth in Texas, Anderson began to craft a story with Roman Coppola, who contributed his own childhood memories (such as his mother Eleanor Coppola using a bullhorn to communicate around the house). The result is something both fantastical and grounded in recognizable childhood experiences, such as being a Cub Scout or taking part in a community theatre production—Anderson himself, as a child, had taken part in a performance of Benjamin Britten's *Noye's Fludde*, the opera that features in this film.

We are introduced to the fictional New Penzance Island through the to-camera monologues of the narrator (Bob Balaban) who also appears to be a resident, having taught Sam cartography. The scenes of the narrator showing off various sights and points of interest position him in front of rather breathtaking scenery, dressed in a striking red peacoat and green hat [OPPOSITE]. His outfit is reminiscent of those from *The Life Aquatic with Steve Zissou*, but also handily draws our attention as audience members. At the film's outset, the location is calm and sunny, defined by large swathes of lush grass and dense woodland. Despite being tiny, the island

#C3C7B2
R195 G199 B178

#BC9E26
R188 158 B38

#840505
R132 G5 B5

#203F37
R32 G63 B55

seems vast and impressive, reflecting the way in which landscapes appear to children, and how memories of places we visited when young appear much grander in our mind's eye.

As in many of his films, Anderson chose to give his main characters vibrant costumes, which they wear for the majority of the film. Suzy's pastel-pink dress [PAGE 96] conveys both her femininity and the desire to be seen as mature, underscored by the bright-blue eyeshadow and black-and-white saddle shoes she pairs it with. Sam's ever-present Khaki Scout uniform [PAGE 97] can be seen as a representation of his desire to belong to a family. He takes great pride in his admirable scouting abilities, even if his peers do not like him.

Sam's ostracization does not seem to matter so much to him after he meets Suzy. He first sees her when wandering backstage at a local production of the children's opera *Noye's Fludde*, in which Suzy plays a raven, resplendent in a black feathered costume [OPPOSITE]. A bird rich with symbolism, the raven is at once an ill-omen and a representation of insight and transformation, which fits with Suzy's mysterious character. Despite having the appearance of a sweet 12-year-old girl, we quickly learn that Suzy struggles with her temper, and has been reprimanded for attacking another student in class. When they meet, and begin their year-long letter correspondence, Suzy and Sam both find a kindred spirit: a safe haven in a storm.

#C8A73A
R200 G167 B58

#8E4C7B
R142 G76 B123

#948884
R148 G136 B132

#0A070A
R10 G7 B10

It is a storm that provides much of the drama in the third act, as the islanders gather in the local church to take shelter from an oncoming gale. Sam and Suzy, running away together for the second time, find themselves sheltering on the roof, dowsed in a blue light [TOP] that reinforces the drama of their intense feelings for one another and the devastation of being kept apart.

Prior to this dramatic weather event, there had been a peaceful calm and sunshine on the island, with Sam and Suzy often positioned within wide shots, emphasizing their smallness against the scenery and, in turn, how the world seems never to be on their side [BOTTOM]. While Sam's scout uniform blends into the surroundings, Suzy's pink dress does not, highlighting the childish impracticality of their running away together in the first place. The weather turns once the adults find and separate Sam and Suzy, playfully suggesting a supernatural element to their love story; once Suzy and Sam are out of peril, the weather returns to the former serenity—albeit with considerable storm damage to the island.

By this point in our journey through Wes Anderson's use of color, perhaps it goes without saying that yellow has a significant role to play in *Moonrise Kingdom*. As well as being the color used for the title font (making this the sixth of 12 Anderson features or shorts thus far to use yellow in the title card), there is a golden patina to the film, which reflects its 1960s setting and the dreamy nostalgia of childhood. There are also a few notable yellow accessories, including the scouting neckerchiefs, [PAGES 102–03, TOP] Suzy's suitcase and the yellow tent that the pair pitch during their escape (reminiscent of Richie's tent in *The Royal Tenenbaums*). Yellow is the thread that connects Anderson's characters together. Although there is no "Wes Anderson Universe," any one of his creations could step quite happily into the world of another, despite the scope of ideas, themes, and settings the filmmaker has chosen over the years. His consistent, careful use of color (and strong championing of shooting on film, which has a distinct grain and texture) has greatly contributed to this feeling of his work as a complete body.

Moonrise Kingdom might first appear to be one of the director's more whimsical films, but the glimpses of violence underscore how cruel children can be to each other (and to themselves). When Suzy attacks Redford, Sam's chief bully, with a pair of scissors, it is a sharply unsettling moment, even if we only see the aftermath (which also features an accidentally murdered dog). Similarly striking is the shot of a burning doghouse in the darkness [PAGES 102–03, BOTTOM]. The strength of the film is how it maintains this balance between child-like optimism and innocence, and the harsh realities of the world. Much in the same way, Anderson's sparing use of darker colors to emphasize moments of tension and peril makes them all the more effective. Unabashedly disinterested in realism and favoring what he can do to turn imagination into reality, here Anderson grants a seriousness and tenderness to a childhood romance and captures something true about the harshness of growing up feeling completely alone in the world. But the story is told with such warmth—both in script and color—that it maintains an effervescence, as only Anderson knows how.

#1C2D7B
R28 G45 B123

#000020
R0 G0 B32

#5698A4
R86 G152 B164

#A27414
R162 G116 B20

#ACAA94
R172 G170 B148

THE AGE OF INNOCENCE

THE GRAND BUDAPEST HOTEL 2014

Wes Anderson's enduring love affair with Europe culminated in the most magical of ways: in 2014, he released *The Grand Budapest Hotel*, widely considered to be not only one of his best films, but one of the greatest of the twenty-first century. It was also his most successful commercially, earning $174.6 million on a $25 million budget, and receiving nine Oscar nominations that brought four wins (notably for costume design, hair and make-up, and production design). The image of the soft-pink facade of the titular hotel [OPPOSITE] is among the most enduring of Anderson's career, and within his filmography, it represented something of a departure from the more woodsy colors of his previous work. But what was it about a caper set in a charming, grandiose hotel in a fictional European country on the brink of war that so enchanted audiences?

Well, Ralph Fiennes for one, as the exacting, fabulously eccentric Gustave H., who serves as the Grand Budapest's concierge. With his pencil moustache, signature cologne (L'Air de Panache), and immaculate royal-purple uniform, Gustave H. is one of Anderson's most memorable characters and among his most fastidious. The particular shade of purple chosen for the hotel's staff uniforms has long been associated with regality and ambition, illustrating the upmarket nature of the business, but it is also a color associated with vanity and frivolity (pairing well with the character of Gustave H.). The purple of the Grand Budapest's uniforms complements the regal crimson of the hotel's luxurious lobby and elevator [PAGE 106] (the same shade we see the elderly Zero wearing at the end of the film), and, of course, the delicate pastel pink of its iconic facade.

#E4B2BE
R228 G178 B190

#8CA6BE
R140 G166 B190

#DA9069
R218 G144 B105

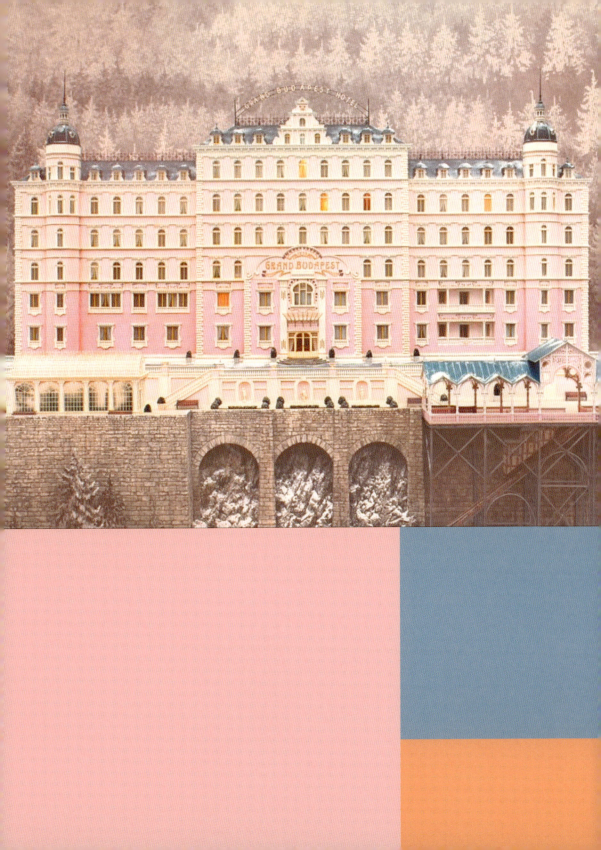

#E0AF79
R224 G175 B121

#FDE8D6
R253 G232 B214

#71516F
R113 G81 B111

#CA3F17
R202 G63 B23

#E4A03E
R228 G160 B62

#E3B09C
R227 G176 B156

#F6D6C2
R246 G214 B196

#9C1414
R156 G20 B20

#EAB1B1
R234 G177 B177

#D25D60
R210 G93 B96

#3C4878
R60 G72 B120

#784B2A
R120 G75 B42

#EA6A00
R234 G106 B0

#FDCF2B
R253 G207 B43

That same shade of pink recurs throughout the film and has become one of the most characteristic colors within the entirety of Anderson's filmography. We first see it on the cover of the book-within-the-film, followed by a spectacular wide shot of the Grand Budapest itself. Then in Madame D.'s suite, where she meets with Gustave H. [PAGE 107], and the boxes delivered by Mendl's Bakery [TOP], drawing a connection between the two establishments. This is further solidified when Gustave's protégé Zero falls in love with the baker's assistant, Agatha, as illustrated in a scene with dreamy orange and yellow lights, out of focus in the background—a photographic effect known as "bokeh" [BOTTOM]. It is the color of first love and delicacy, suggesting innocence and elegance. It is notable that, when we see the hotel years later, the lobby has been remodelled for the 1960s, instead sporting orange and yellow interiors. At the same time, the film's color grading in the secondary timeline is less densely saturated, indicating not only the Grand Budapest's gradual decline, but the tragic death of Zero's beloved Agatha.

In sharp contrast to the playful colors of the Grand Budapest and its staff, the villains of the film—namely Adrien Brody's Dmitri Desgoffe-und-Taxis and Willem Dafoe's J. G. Jopling—dress in black [PAGES 110–11, TOP]. This might be an obvious choice to denote their nefariousness, but it is certainly an effective one, illustrating how the characters stand out against the hotel and signal oncoming trouble. This follows in the form of the police and soldiers who are eventually stationed within the Grand Budapest at Dmitri's behest, sporting gray uniforms under the black banner of Zubrowka (it is no mistake their logo closely resembles the double sig rune used by the Schutzstaffel during the Second World War).

The concierge who replaces Gustave—M. Chuck, played by Owen Wilson—sports a hotel uniform in the same color, a warning sign of things to come. For a brief while, even Gustave H. dresses in gray, after he is incarcerated—though he manages to make it look fairly stylish [BOTTOM].

The use of black and gray occurs in one other scene: a flashback that takes place after the events of the main storyline and that depicts the moment Gustave H. is killed on a train by fascist soldiers while defending Zero. It is the most violent and tragic moment of the film—a sharp departure from the relative frivolity that otherwise defines *The Grand Budapest Hotel*, which makes it all the more effective.

A critique often levelled at Anderson's films is that they are "style over substance," and that his meticulous eye for detail and physical construction papers over narrative flaws. *The Grand Budapest Hotel* is a powerful rejoinder to this argument—the style *is* the substance. The rich, bold colors of the film's 1930s timeline speak to the opulence of the setting and the seeming frivolity of its caper storyline, but these are undercut by the looming threat of war and fascist oppression. It is perhaps Anderson's most tragic film, in which a lonely man who has suffered quite endlessly in life recounts his story with a powerful stoicism and nostalgic glint in his eye. Of course, in Zero's mind the colours of The Grand Budapest are brightest during the 1930s, when Gustave and Agatha are still alive, and he is the bright-eyed lobby boy who had escaped certain death. But as L. P. Hartley wrote in *The Go-Between*—another story of a young outsider thrust into the world of the upper class—"The past is a foreign country; they do things differently there."

#0A0A0A
R10 G10 B10

#A36825
R163 G103 B37

#877E78
R135 G126 B120

#A59E9E
R165 G158 B158

#646973
R100 G105 B115

#96747C
R150 G116 B124

Wes Anderson has never been shy about his cinematic inspirations. He is seemingly a voracious reader, art appreciator, and scholar of cinema, and watching his interviews can be dizzying, due to the sheer volume of artistic references he draws on at any given moment.

While making *Bottle Rocket* with Owen Wilson, right at the start of his career, it seems probable that Anderson was inspired by the likes of filmmakers Quentin Tarantino (who had just made *Reservoir Dogs*; 1992) and Martin Scorsese (who would, by chance, later name *Bottle Rocket* one of his favorite films of the 1990s). Although the color palettes have very little in common, the quippy dialogue, crime dramedy plot, and bickering male protagonists certainly seem familiar. Anderson even uses a Rolling Stones song on the soundtrack ("2000 Man"), as Scorsese had in *Mean Streets* (1973; "Jumpin' Jack Flash").

Perhaps an even bigger debt is owed to Jean-Luc Godard, who has been a notable influence on Anderson throughout his career. His own 1964 heist movie *Bande à part*, in which three young adults plot a robbery, was noted for its sense of humor and charm—features that have become staples of Anderson's filmography. French cinema (especially the French New Wave) has been a huge inspiration on the filmmaker's sensibilities, and he regularly cites François Truffaut, Jacques Tati, Jacques Demy, Robert Bresson, and Agnès Varda among his favorite filmmakers of all time. Although Anderson has never made a musical, the bright pastels of Jacques Demy's *The Umbrellas of Cherbourg* (1964) and *The Young Girls of Rochefort* (1967) are an undeniable touchstone for Anderson's own visual style. The absurdism of Jacques Tati's greatest creation, Monsieur Hulot, (who appeared in four of his films) seems to be reflected in the "quirky" characters of Anderson's filmography and, directly, in the opening of *The French Dispatch*, when a waiter delivers drinks to the newspaper's office—as well as the 2008 SoftBank commercial he made with Brad Pitt (see page 90).

American cinema has also had a profound influence on Anderson, with him citing Orson Welles' *The Magnificent Ambersons* (1942) as a direct reference for *The Royal Tenenbaums*. There is definitely a similarity between the extravagant Amberson mansion and 111 Archer Avenue where the Tenenbaum family reside, and both films begin with an introductory narration (Alec Baldwin in *The Royal Tenenbaums*, Orson Welles in *The Magnificent Ambersons*). The character of Alain Leroy in Louis Malle's *The Fire Within* (1963) was also a frame of reference for Richie Tenenbaum, and Martin Scorsese's little-known short *The Big Shave* (1967) seems to be a direct reference for the staging and execution of his suicide attempt. Although, in the director's commentary for the film, it was the "blood and guts" realism of Robert Altman's *M*A*S*H* (1970) that Anderson referred to as an inspiration. Coincidentally, one of Scorsese's favorite films—Powell and Pressburger's *The Red Shoes* (1948)—was also a direct influence on the beginning of *The Royal Tenenbaums*, both featuring a book in the opening sequence. The brightly saturated colors of Powell and Pressburger's oeuvre suggest another key to unlocking the wider world of Anderson's films.

Mike Nichols is another key inspiration on Anderson. This is most evident in *Rushmore*, which owes much to Nichols' *The Graduate* (1967)—to the extent that there is a very similar shot in both films, where the protagonist is peering into a fishtank. More unlikely is the reference to Michael Mann's *Heat* (1995), when

WES WIDE WORLD

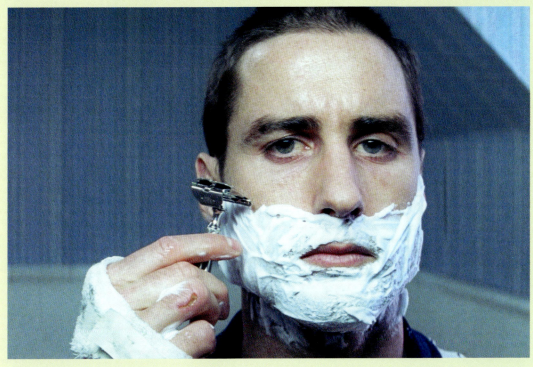

Luke Wilson as Richie Tenenbaum in *The Royal Tenenbaums*

Martin Scorsese's short film *The Big Shave*

Max asks for a dynamite purchase to be billed to Tucson, Arizona (as Val Kilmer does in Mann's film). *Rushmore* also owes a debt to François Truffaut's *The 400 Blows* (1959), as do *Moonrise Kingdom* and the student protest storyline of *The French Dispatch*, indicating that, for Anderson, some obsessions are enduring, popping up in different ways across his work.

The cinema of Satyajit Ray and Yasujirō Ozu are also key influences on Anderson, particularly his portrayal of complex familial relationships. While plenty of music from Satyajit Ray's films features in *The Darjeeling Limited*, the vehicle of a family trip as a narrative conceit owes something to Ozu's *Tokyo Story*.

Beyond film, music has had a significant impact on Anderson's cinema, particularly that of the British bands of his youth, including the Rolling Stones, the Faces, and the Kinks. Jarvis Cocker, of Britpop mainstay Pulp, has also become a close friend and collaborator of Anderson's, appearing in several films, including *Fantastic Mr. Fox* and *Asteroid City*, as well as contributing music to his soundtracks. Dance sequences—from *Moonrise Kingdom*'s (*Badlands*-inspired) beach boogie to *The French Dispatch*'s Demyesque romantic moment between Zeffirelli and Juliette—underscore the importance for Anderson of connection through music, allowing characters to express themselves without the use of language.

The world of fine art has also shaped Wes' filmography, perhaps most evidently in *Isle of Dogs*, which is heavily influenced by the work of Edo-period artist Katsushika Hokusai and the postmodernism of animator Hideaki Anno. But arguably the most famous work of art within a Wes Anderson film is *Boy with Apple*, from *The Grand Budapest Hotel*—a fictional Renaissance painting attributed to Johannes Van Hoytl the Younger, but actually painted by Michael Taylor, inspired by Flemish and German painters, including Hans Holbein the Younger and Pieter Bruegel the Elder. These artists were particularly chosen in contrast to the more popular Italian Renaissance artists, in keeping with the film's setting. Meanwhile, Rich Pellegrino was commissioned to produce another painting, in the style of Egon Schiele, entitled *Two Lesbians Masturbating*, which would become a key misdirection within the film.

The French Dispatch, a loving cinematic tribute to *The New Yorker* magazine and the art of print journalism, features just as much artistic detail, with Anderson enlisting artists Sandro Kopp, Sian Smith, and Edith Baudrand to create an entire back catalogue for fictional artist Moses Rosenthaler, including a series of 3.6-meter frescos in dazzling orange and red. While the work of Frank Auerbach, Willem de Kooning, Francis Bacon, and Félix Vallotton inspired the team in their creations, they were careful to avoid nakedly referencing existing artists. "We were very clear that we needed the paintings to be idiosyncratic and we didn't want the art to look too much like the work of any living or dead painter," Kopp explained to *Dazed* magazine in 2021.

This is barely scratching the surface of Anderson's artistic inspirations, which his dedicated fans still unpack and theorize about. Beyond visual motifs and musical cues, Anderson's films frequently include small cinematic easter eggs for the dedicated fan, making each film a puzzle box of references and tributes. This could be as simple as a character's name (Tilda Swinton's Madame D. in *The Grand Budapest Hotel* is named after the title of Max Ophüls' 1953 romance) or a line referencing another film (such as Zissou saying, "Not this one, Klaus," in *The Life Aquatic*, referencing *Jules et Jim*). It is Anderson's refusal to draw a line between "high" and "'low" art that makes his films such a joy to watch. You are as likely to find a reference to Peter Weir's *Witness* (1985) as you are an homage to abstract artist Mark Rothko. But as inspired as Anderson is by other artists from every corner of the creative world, his films would not be as magical as they are were it not for his own extraordinary imagination. Pablo Picasso said it best: "Good artists copy, great artists steal." Like the quote-unquote *Fantastic Mr. Fox*, Anderson is adept at spotting what to take and how to use it, and the result is something rich and rewarding in its own right.

Establishing shot of newspaper offices in *The French Dispatch*

The house in *Mon Oncle* that inspired the building design in *The French Dispatch*

THE DOG DAYS ARE OVER

ISLE OF DOGS
2018

After the adventure of creating a stop-motion feature film in *Fantastic Mr. Fox*, Anderson returned to the world of animation a decade later, this time crafting an original story with help from Roman Coppola, Jason Schwartzman, and Kunichi Nomura. As a lifelong fan of Japanese cinema and frequent traveler to the country, it seemed inevitable that, at some point, Anderson would make a film there, though perhaps no one could have known he would take "make" quite so literally. *Isle of Dogs* takes place in the near future, in the fictional Japanese metropolis of Megasaki, where a dog-hating mayoral dynasty has a scheme to wipe out man's best friend once and for all. It was shot using elaborate puppets and miniatures, as well as some cartoon sequences.

Amid the chaos, *Isle of Dogs* is primarily a story about a young boy trying to find his lost pet. Twelve-year-old Atari Kobayashi flies to Trash Island after his beloved dog Spots is exiled there, as part of a mayoral decree banning dogs within the city. It is here that he meets a motley crew of mutts, each a beautifully designed puppet, and together they embark on an adventure not only to reunite Atari and Spots, but also to resist the might of the mayor's office altogether.

As with *Fantastic Mr. Fox*, Anderson and his team (primarily production designers Paul Harrod and Adam Stockhausen, and art director Curt Enderle, plus a host of designers and artists) created elaborate miniature sets and models to shoot with, allowing for an incredible level of detail and world-building. Where *Fantastic Mr. Fox* was immersed in the world that Roald Dahl so vividly described, here the minds of Anderson and co ran wild, drawing inspiration from the likes of Katsushika Hokusai, Hayao Miyazaki, Katsuhiro Otomo, Akira Kurosawa, and Rankin/Bass' classic Holiday Specials to create something recognizable as a futuristic version of Japan, but also visually engrossing and unique.

The sprawling cityscape of Megasaki and Trash Island, where the dogs are exiled, are distinct. Megasaki is mostly shot at night (where twinkling buildings light up the skyline [TOP], giving it a futuristic glow), or through interiors, from the sunny yellow of the Megasaki Senior High newspaper office and a warmly lit ramen shop full of pint-sized baseball players to the lavishly pro-cat compound of the devilish Mayor Kobayashi [BOTTOM]. Meanwhile, Trash Island is . . . made of trash, albeit in an aesthetically pleasing fashion, compacted into silver-gray cubes piled high into makeshift mountains. The sky is a bright white, which is particularly unusual

#B42A1E
R180 G42 B30

#673E36
R103 G62 B54

#E1CE4A
R225 G206 B74

#AE261A
R174 G38 B26

#5C3F85
R92 G63 B133

#9EBCB4
R158 G188 B180

#7DBB00
R125 G187 B0

#FAEB00
R250 G235 B0

#DC782D
R220 G120 B45

for the color-loving Anderson, but this sparsity allows the design of the puppets to take center stage [PAGES 118–119, TOP]. The most prominent of these is Chief (voiced by Bryan Cranston), a black stray dog with piercing blue eyes and white spots, who has a particular distrust of humans. Each mutt has its own distinct design imbued with personality. There is Duke, a gray-and-white husky breed, then Boss, who sports a baseball shirt as a proud mascot, and Nutmeg, a "show dog" with silky smooth, sand-colored fur. As well as affording more space for the puppets to stand out, the stark white also hints at the limbo the dogs have been placed in, not yet dead, not really alive, and the physical distance that has grown between man and man's best friend.

But the island is not totally devoid of color. There are structures the dogs have managed to build, as well as some abandoned buildings from previous human occupation. Anderson shoots a particularly striking scene inside a refuge made from colored glass bottles, utilizing shadow to create a strong sense of visual contrast between the soft shapes of the dogs and the hard glass in the background [PAGES 118–19, BOTTOM]. The playful use of shadow throughout *Isle of Dogs* appears to be a tribute to the art of shadow puppetry, which is particularly popular in Asia. More widely, the film owes visual inspiration to the Japanese art of *bunraku*, a traditional form of Japanese puppetry (the film is bookended by a scene of children using taiko drums, a key feature of *bunraku*).

The colors and textures of science fiction naturally also have a place within the film, from Atari's silver flight suit [OPPOSITE] to the menacing robot-dogs that are dispatched to attack the real canines, reminiscent of Mechagodzilla (*Godzilla vs. Mechagodzilla*, 1974). These metals and metallics contrast against the glimpses we get of the natural world, hinted at in brilliant orange sunsets and sandy dunes in the distance [PAGES 122–23].

Despite Anderson's clear affection for Japan, it should be acknowledged that *Isle of Dogs* attracted criticism on release, notably for the relegation of Japanese characters to supporting roles in a film purportedly about them (all the dogs "spoke" English, played by American and British actors). While Moeko Fujii wrote a favorable review in *The New Yorker*, praising the director's consideration of the boundaries of language, in the *Los Angeles Times*, Justin Chang remarked, "It's in the director's handling of the story's human factor that his sensitivity falters, and the weakness for racial stereotyping that has sometimes marred his work comes to the fore."

Yet the artistry within *Isle of Dogs* is still evident, and Anderson's use of color to bring a futuristic fictional world to life is evocative. At its heart, the film is a love story, about the lengths a boy is willing to go to for his dog—and the love that is returned to him along the way. This sentiment contrasts with the stark, metallic colors that the film favors, creating a playful juxtaposition between a sweet message and steely *mise-en-scène*.

#5F7AAE
R95 G122 B174

#B44C3C
R180 G76 B60

#C6BEB8
R198 G190 B184

NEWS OF THE WORLD

THE FRENCH DISPATCH
2021

Born out of Wes Anderson's enduring love for print journalism, and in particular, *The New Yorker* magazine, *The French Dispatch* is an anthology film about the last edition of the eponymous publication: an outpost of the *Liberty, Kansas Evening Sun* based in the sleepy fictional French town Ennui-sur-Blasé in the mid-twentieth century [TOP]. While the town itself is presented as charmingly situated but fairly gray and drab, the same can't be said of its occupants. With its eccentric cast of characters, multiple storylines and use of both black-and-white and color film (as well as cartoons in its final segment), *The French Dispatch* is idiosyncratic even by Wes Anderson's exacting standards. It is certainly a feast for the eyes, instantly transporting viewers to the lived-in, dreamy world of a dedicated team of journalists and their equally absorbing subjects, tied together by the bright yellow magazine office where they all convene [BOTTOM].

Opening with a eulogy for the recently deceased editor-in-chief Arthur Howitzer Jr., read by narrator Anjelica Huston, the film unfolds in four stories told by four reporters: travel writer Herbsaint Sazerac's short "local color" guide to Ennui-sur-Blasé; arts' writer J. K. L. Berensen's "The Concrete Masterpiece," about outsider artist Moses Rosenthaler; Lucinda Krementz's "Revisions to a Manifesto," a report on the student revolutionaries led by Zeffirelli; and food writer Roebuck Wright's "The Private Dining Room of the Police Commissioner," recalling the kidnapping of a police commissioner's son and the revolutionary work of famous police officer and chef Nescaffier.

In discussing how color informed the stories with *British Cinematographer* magazine, Anderson's regular cinematographer Robert Yeoman explained: "Wes wanted each one to have a very specific look, so they would appear to have been written by different writers." To do this, Yeoman and Anderson vary the use of color and black-and-white in each section [PAGE 126] and switch up the framing (Berensen delivers her story as a lecture; Wright as a television interview [PAGE 127]). While some critics have remarked that the black-and-white scenes could indicate what is in the written version of the story and the color scenes are what the writers left out, things are not quite as clear-cut as this. Perhaps, instead, the black-and-white segments indicate the memories the writers have of the story, rather than the printed version. Or perhaps there is no concrete methodology, and color was simply used—as it so often is within cinema—to draw our attention to something.

#466A7D
R70 G106 B125

#A59682
R165 G150 B130

#99723A
R153 G114 B58

#B7450A
R183 G69 B10

#AFBCAF
R175 G188 B175

#8A783A
R138 G120 B58

#412822
R65 G40 B34

#8C4434
R140 G68 B52

#D8D8D8
R216 G216 B216

#8C8C8C
R140 G140 B140

#5A5A5A
R90 G90 B90

#161616
R22 G22 B22

In any case, the mixture works well. In "The Concrete Masterpiece," color is used primarily for shots of Rosenthaler's paintings, which emphasizes their magnitude—bright pinks and reds against orange concrete walls [TOP]. Yeoman was inspired by Richard Brooks' adaptation of Truman Capote's *In Cold Blood* (1967) for the black-and-white scenes of Rosenthaler in prison; these naturally lack the freedom and creativity of his art, and reinforce the harshness of the environment Rosenthaler is confined to.

Naturally, the French New Wave provided ample inspiration for the film as well, notably Jean-Luc Godard's *Diabolique* (1955) and *Vivre sa vie* (1962); the film's 1:37:1 aspect ratio reflects the influence. But the most striking moment of "Revisions to a Manifesto" is surely when the entire set of Le Sans Blague café opens up on to the street, evoking the dreamscapes of musical maestro Jacques Tati. Anderson shoots this sequence in colou, not quite Tati's memorable pastels, but a neon-lit jukebox is a time-appropriate substitute. We then watch as Zeffirelli and Juliette cruise off on her motorcycle, doused in blue light [BOTTOM], reflecting the adolescent thrill of blossoming romance.

"The Private Dining Room of the Police Commissioner" utilizes black and white the most out of the segments, with color only appearing as Roebuck recounts the story on a talk show, when Nescaffier delivers his much-anticipated menu, and in one shot where the young Gigi asks the showgirl minding his door what color her eyes are. Perhaps Anderson chooses this moment to emphasize a spark of humanity amid a fairly callous kidnapping. Similarly, the use of black and white when Roebuck recounts his own imprisonment for homosexuality seems to reflect Rosenthaler's incarceration from earlier in the film. The use of color in the scenes with food [PAGE 130] seems clear, emphasizing the ceremony of Nescaffier's dishes and how fondly Roebuck recalls the experience. Of the three segments, this final one is the most tender, largely due to Jeffrey Wright's astonishing performance as Roebuck Wright, but the mixed use of color and monochrome also feels best suited here.

Generally well received, *The French Dispatch* is arguably among the most "Wes Anderson" Wes Anderson films, combining so many of his interests and passions as to be something of a complex beast. The director delivers arresting images: the bright-yellow facade of the Le Sans Blague café [PAGE 131] is among the strongest in his oeuvre. Brimming with ideas and lovingly crafted in its off-kilter structure, Anderson's tribute to the world of culture journalism might be destined to remain a less popular part of his oeuvre, but it is evident that he poured his heart and soul into making it, infusing the film with his enthusiasm for print journalism. The experimental combination of color with black-and-white would serve him well when making *Asteroid City*.

#BC6E6C
R188 G110 B108

#C59700
R197 G151 B0

#BBB09A
R187 G176 B154

#5DA7DE
R93 G167 B222

#2A3C8C
R42 G60 B140

#0B0B0E
R11 G11 B14

DRAWING STARS

"ALINE" MUSIC VIDEO 2021

It is somewhat surprising that Wes Anderson had not made a music video before teaming up with Jarvis Cocker for "Aline," considering this is how many of his contemporaries—including Spike Jonze, David Fincher, and Sofia Coppola—got their start. He is certainly no stranger to commercial filmmaking pursuits. Yet, for whatever reason, it was not until *The French Dispatch* had finished production that Anderson decided to make his music-video debut. He directed a hand-drawn, animated video to accompany a cover of French singer Christophe's "Aline," performed by Jarvis Cocker as the fictitious French musician Tip-Top, who appears in the feature film.

Anderson approached Javi Aznarez for the job—the artist had already designed *The New Yorker*-inspired illustrations for *The French Dispatch*—and it took him (plus a team of seven) eight months to complete the three-minute video. It shows Cocker, as Tip-Top, strolling through the town of Ennui-sur-Blasé while singing, giving us a glimpse of both the setting for the film and some of the characters who appear within it. It functions almost like an atlas—placing each panel side by side would create "one giant fresco of the entire town," as explained by producer Octavia Peissel in an interview about the project with online file-sharing site WeTransfer.

Perhaps even more surprising is the fact that the music video has a very sparse use of color, with most of the drawings rendered in black and white; it could not be more different from *The French Dispatch*. The effect creates the sensation that the music video is a newspaper cartoon strip that has come to life, complete with the requisite Wes Anderson level of detail. It also means that what small pockets of color are used really stand out—Tip-Top's yellow suit with orange shirt [OPPOSITE], a bundle of baguettes in the back of a car, and the violins and tubas of the prison band that the singer strolls or cycles past [PAGE 134].

Also rendered in color are the film's characters positioned throughout the video. We see Frances McDormand's Lucinda Krementz and Timothée Chalamet's Zeffirelli hanging out at Le Sans Blague café with its bright-yellow facade, for example [PAGE 135]. There is even a blink-and-you'll-miss-it Wes Anderson cameo; he plays a delivery driver at the wheel of a French Dispatch van chugging up a hill. The video is at once something quite different for Wes Anderson, and perfectly in keeping with the film it accompanies: a meticulously crafted tribute to Ennui-sur-Blasé.

● #1A1E1E R26 G30 B30
#FAFAF4 R250 G250 B244
◐ #DED476 R222 G212 B118
● #D48232 R212 G130 B50

It all started with Dignan's jumpsuit in *Bottle Rocket*. Banana yellow, as Future Man (played by Owen Wilson's older brother Andrew) astutely observes. "He looks like a little banana," Future Man snorts. But Dignan digs the yellow jumpsuit (perhaps a nod to Bruce Lee's iconic outfit from 1978's *Game of Death*) and stipulates that their gang should all wear them to carry out the heist at the cold-storage facility. It might seem totally impractical to don extremely identifying yellow jumpsuits for a break-in, but the outfit choice seems indicative of several key personality traits in Dignan: his flair for dramatics, his oddball nature, and, crucially, his desire to belong to a tribe. He talks incessantly about Mr. Henry for the first part of the film, clearly in awe of him, desperate to be part of his crew. In managing to convince members to wear yellow jumpsuits for their big score, Dignan has created his own family.

Throughout the films of Wes Anderson, no color has had the staying power of yellow. From the bright goldenrod of Richie Tenenbaum's childhood tent in *The Royal Tenenbaums* to the yellow submarine in *The Life Aquatic with Steve Zissou* (most obviously a reference to the Beatles), the color features in significant ways across the director's filmography, and although the shades might shift with the meaning, once you notice it, there is no forgetting it.

The most "yellow" film is arguably *Fantastic Mr. Fox*, where the fall color palette evokes the countryside setting, with striking sunsets and rustic 1960s Britain styling, in keeping with the time period in which Roald Dahl wrote the original novel (first published in 1970). Mr. Fox's signature shirt is a butter color, while his wife Felicity wears a yellow dress with a pattern of red apples, indicating their synchronicity. (It should be noted that the lead farmer, Frank Bean, also has a yellow shirt—maybe he and Foxy are not so different after all.) Much of the film also seems to take place in golden hour—not just because foxes are crepuscular creatures. It is a known fact that golden hour produces some of the most covetable natural light, and mimicking this in stop-motion is quite a coup, creating a sense of nostalgia and whimsy purely through the use of color.

Yellow as the color of nostalgia also informs *The Royal Tenenbaums* and *Moonrise Kingdom*, which have distinctly golden tones to their palettes. While Richie Tenenbaum's childhood tent in *The Royal Tenenbaums* was directly inspired by Jean-Pierre Melville's *Les Enfants terribles* (1950; which also, more broadly, inspired the relationship between Margot and Richie), it seems as though Sam Shakusky's tent in *Moonrise Kingdom* was a reference to Richie's—perhaps a symbol of childhood defiance and the desire to escape.

WES AND YELLOW

Dignan sporting his banana yellow jumpsuit in *Bottle Rocket*

But yellow is almost as common in *Moonrise Kingdom* as it is in *Fantastic Mr. Fox*. Here, yellow is the color of innocence and youth, and in particular youthful defiance. In Suzy Bishop's suitcase and Sam's neckerchief, it seems to represent an idealistic determination.

But do not be fooled into thinking there is a unifying theory that links Anderson's use of yellow. While it is a recurring color in the filmmaker's work, the shades and meaning shift, depending on the film. For example, the use of yellow in *The Life Aquatic with Steve Zissou*—as both the color of Zissou's submarine and of the elusive jaguar shark—indicates that there is more of a connection between the two than Zissou initially thought.

But this does not necessarily tie the film to, say, *The Darjeeling Limited*, and *Hotel Chevalier* and the yellow of Jack Whitman's hotel robe. While it does often feel as though any one of Anderson's characters could easily step between his worlds, his films are not made to exist within one universe.

Sometimes, yellow is simply the color that creates the biggest visual impact. This is true of *Isle of Dogs*, where Tracy Walker's blonde afro creates a more cohesive contrast to the black, white, and gray color palette of the film. The same could be said for yellow in *The French Dispatch*, where it dominates as the color of the magazine's offices and of Le Sans Blague café, offering the greatest contrast between the black-and-white film sequences and those in color.

Perhaps, on some level, Anderson's penchant for the color yellow comes from growing up in Houston, Texas, where even winter is balmy compared to much of the United States. Yellow is the color of sun-parched grass, of long sunsets and lazy sunrises. It was also, coincidentally, the color of the walls in Roald Dahl's writing shed, lovingly recreated in Anderson's *The Wonderful Story of Henry Sugar and Three More*. It permeates Anderson's short films here, notably *The Rat Catcher*, where the very sky is painted an odd, unearthly yellow, perhaps reflecting the story's fantastical conceit.

The beauty of color comes from its shifting meaning across cultures, time periods and individuals. While yellow is generally associated with feelings of joy and excitement, it is also a color used for warning signs, to indicate caution, and as a symbol of cowardice. Despite the prevalence of the color in the films of Wes Anderson, the meaning is fluid and privy to personal interpretation.

That said . . . it is no secret that Wes himself loves yellow. A post on blogging site Tumblr documents him wearing the same yellow scarf both on and off set across a period of at least five years. Given that nothing is left to chance in a Wes Anderson film, there is intention and thought behind every use of yellow, regardless of how fleeting it may be in the grand scheme of things. But no two yellows are created alike, and Anderson's films encourage us to look closer, interrogating our own feelings as well as those of the characters we are watching. The yellow tents of Richie Tenenbaum and Sam Shakusky might represent childlike optimism, but to some extent, they also represent cowardice and a desire to retreat from the real world into something more naive and safer.

The bold, eye-catching nature of this primary color means we cannot help but pay attention. The arid desert yellows of *Asteroid City* remind us we are in a lonely place, but also one that brims with scientific possibility. One thing is for certain: yellow is never *just* yellow. Regardless of the conclusions we draw as individuals, it is clear that Anderson's use of the color is a sort of Rorschach test, encouraging us to find our own deeper meaning, and embrace the joy, anxiety, and energy in between.

The shrine to Zeffirelli outside Le Sans Blague café in *The French Dispatch*

Mr. and Mrs Fox in their matching yellow outfits in *Fantastic Mr. Fox*

WRITTEN IN THE STARS

ASTEROID CITY
2023

Wes Anderson has always held plenty of stock in all things fantastical, yet his live-action films have hewn closer to the "realism" side of "magical realism," while retaining a fairytale quality that seems indicative of his expansive imagination and love of playful details. *Asteroid City*, then, is something of a departure: presented as a televized play with two storylines unfolding in parallel (on the screen and behind the scenes), it is at once a sci-fi epic and a grounded story of performers and performance. It is also (following on from Anderson's and Robert Yeoman's work on *The French Dispatch*) shot in both black-and-white and colou, to differentiate between the reality of the play and the onscreen narrative.

The play-within-the-film concerns a science summit for junior stargazers, primarily focused on the Steenbeck family, led by their morose and serious patriarch Augie, who is played by lead character Jones Hall (Jason Schwartzman) in the parallel "real world" storyline. His eldest child Woodrow (Jake Ryan) and the other junior stargazers, as well as their families and guests, are shocked when an alien interrupts their festivities and steals (or rather, borrows) the town's prized asteroid.

Asteroid City is, perhaps, Anderson's most colorful film, shot against the arid Spanish plains that stand in for the fictional American desert town "allegedly somewhere in the California/Nevada/Arizona desert" (per the screenplay) that gives the film its name. The bright-blue skies with perfect cotton-wool clouds and orange-brown dirt punctuated by large rocks and stubborn green cacti resemble the memorable backgrounds from Looney Tunes' Road Runner and Wile E. Coyote cartoons [OPPOSITE]. There is even a little road runner who appears intermittently throughout the film, a knowing reference to the most enduring American image of the strangeness of the desert. The heat, which is the first thing movie star Midge Campbell (Scarlett Johansson, also playing actress Mercedes Ford) remarks upon when stepping out of her car, is palpable, and through one gorgeous tracking shot in the opening scene, we are taken on a silent tour of the town's (extremely few) landmarks. This immediately creates a sense of place, and combined with the vivid choice of colors, the audience is instantly drawn into this fantastical setting.

In extreme contrast, the external world of *Asteroid City*—which shows the development of the play by Conrad Earp (Edward Norton) through to its televisation—is shot in the black and white of an old television set. General Grif Gibson's reference to his father fighting in "the war to end all wars" and the atom bomb

#F2E6AF
R242 G230 B175

#265F87
R38 G95 B135

#E0B074
R224 G176 B116

#5EBBB4
R94 G187 B180

tests taking place just beyond Asteroid City place the play in the mid-1950s (confirmed by a note on Anderson's screenplay). This informs the choice of particularly bright colors for the film, reflecting the advent of color film, which seems even brighter when interspersed with the black-and-white segments.

The lack of shadow in this desert adds an uncanny element to *Asteroid City*, enhancing its positioning as a fiction-within-a-fiction. Even by Wes Anderson's standards, where his films frequently appear as lovingly crafted dioramas and dollhouses, there is a choreography to the play's storyline. As Robert Yeoman noted in an interview with Focus Features film studio, "Wes was eager to use the sun as a kind of a character in the film" [BOTTOM].

This contrasts with the use of shadow and light within the behind-the-scenes narrative, where the tragic circumstances of Earp's death (and Jones Hall's mourning for him) loom large, as well as the divorce of the play's director Schubert Green (Adrien Brody, channelling Elia Kazan and Arthur Miller) and his spat with lead actress Mercedes Ford. The latter has the look of Marilyn Monroe about her [PAGES 142–43, BOTTOM]. In backstage scenes, we also see real pieces of the *Asteroid City* set, used after the "film" scenes had been shot, further creating the sense that we are watching a play-within-a-film.

The styling and colous of characters within Asteroid City are as exacting as ever. Augie's beige ensemble [PAGES 142–43, TOP] is reminiscent of Jane Winslett-Richardson's from *The Life Aquatic*; like her, he is a journalist (a war photographer) but the attachment to the outfit even off duty suggests an inability to separate himself from his work. In his black-and-white scenes as Jones Hall [TOP], he is styled after James Dean—particularly Phil Stern's 1955 portrait, where his face is partially obscured by his sweater. Here the lack of color is just as important, making the connection between Hall and Dean much more obvious.

We also have an example of Anderson and Yeoman using coloued gels to set a scene apart from the rest of the film, as in *The French Dispatch*'s motorcycle ride. Here, it is the climactic scene in which the alien arrives in Asteroid City. The alien's ship casts the crater in an otherworldly green hue, and the humans stare up at the sky, transfixed. The alien—a puppet brilliantly brought to life in a similar fashion to the characters in *Fantastic Mr. Fox* and *Isle of Dogs*—is tall and skinny, with white eyes and a black spacesuit [PAGES 146–47]. It has a familiar shape (like the aliens of 1977's *Close Encounters of the Third Kind*, another *Asteroid City* touchstone) but the alien's big eyes and cautious cat-like movements give it a much cuter appearance than we are used to seeing from extraterrestrials, in keeping with the fact that the alien means the humans no harm.

Amid the out-of-the-ordinary, there also exists the mundane. A retro American diner [TOP] and a mechanic's workshop are two of the small businesses that manage to stay afloat in town; naturally, they are rendered in

#D7D0BE
R215 G208 B190

#161614
R22 G22 B20

#64625C
R100 G98 B92

#BCF9D8
R188 G249 B216

#F5FCD2
R245 G252 B210

#988A6C
R152 G138 B108

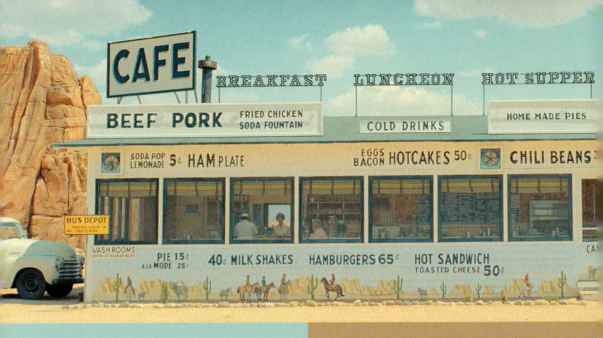

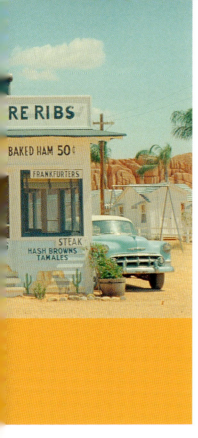

#8CD0C6
R140 G208 B198

#B48C5E
R180 G140 B94

#DE9C0D
R222 G156 B13

classic 1950s style. Even the red glacé cherry atop Woodrow's milkshake seems particularly perfect, and the military's meticulous planning of the Junior Stargazer's Convention speaks to the particular hold that the armed forces had over American popular culture in the postwar period, before the Vietnam War sowed seeds of mistrust among citizens. Even the set of brightly colored vending machines at the back of the motel (one of which, quite delightfully, serves a perfect martini with a twist [BOTTOM]) seem indicative of the optimism of the time, but the film does not necessarily yearn for the past. Hints of the failure of the American dream (atom tests, the military attempting to take ownership of the inventions of the young scientists, the vending machine selling off portions of the desert as real estate for $10 a piece) all lead back to the question Jones Hall desperately asks Schubert Green during the play's third act: "Am I doing him right?"

This anxiety is the central theme of the film, not just limited to Jones' fear of not doing justice to Conrad's script in the wake of his death. We see it in Augie's reluctance to tell his children about their mother's passing, in Midge's insecurities around her career, in Woodrow's nervousness around the other students, and in the disastrous attempts by the military to cover up the alien encounter altogether. Fear—particularly fear of the unknown—is a universal experience, and *Asteroid City* suggests that the only way to overcome it is simply to carry on moving, like a train on a track. The sun goes on shining regardless, so we might as well move with it. There are wonders out there far beyond our comprehension; sometimes it's enough to simply bear witness.

#709C7B
R112 G156 B123

#DAB640
R218 G182 B64

#969682
R150 G150 B130

SEEING GOOD

THE WONDERFUL STORY OF HENRY SUGAR
2023

When Netflix acquired the rights to Roald Dahl's body of work in 2021, it seemed extremely likely that a raft of new adaptations would be on the way. Instead, the streaming service made a smart decision in hiring Wes Anderson for its first foray into Dahl, no doubt the result of his long-standing connection to the author. Perhaps less expected was the project Anderson announced in 2022: an adaptation of the lesser-known Dahl work *The Wonderful Story of Henry Sugar*, a short-story collection from 1977. Sometime later, before the film premiered at the Venice Film Festival, Anderson confirmed it was a 40-minute short film, and that he had also adapted three other Roald Dahl stories (*The Swan*, *The Rat Catcher*, and *Poison*) using the same compact cast and theater-influenced staging.

Although not feature length, *The Wonderful Story of Henry Sugar* is still twice as long as the other shorts and is set across the globe, from Dahl's house in Buckinghamshire to the Indian jungle. Benedict Cumberbatch plays the titular role, as a bored rich man who becomes obsessed with learning clairvoyance after stumbling across an account of an Indian man who had achieved just that. In the process, Sugar becomes a better person, realizing that he has been quite selfish, and vows to help the less fortunate with his remarkable new gift.

The story begins in a recreation of Dahl's famous writing shed, located in his garden, with Ralph Fiennes starring as the writer (possibly inspired by a televised interview on BBC's *Pebble Mill at One* in 1982) and explaining how he gets ready to write [OPPOSITE]. The bright-yellow walls and Dahl's red shirt are taken from reality, albeit styled in the symmetrical, aesthetically pleasing manner to which Anderson is accustomed. There is a coziness to the opening, which contrasts with the scenes of Henry Sugar's extravagant but comparatively empty life at the start of the story. His apartment is lavish, but spartan; he dresses well, albeit without much personality. While snooping around a library at a boring party, Henry discovers an interesting book titled *The Man Who Could See Without His Eyes*.

We enter a story-within-a-story, which is set up like a play, with moving, highly decorated sets (it seems likely Anderson was inspired by his experiences shooting *Asteroid City*, and perhaps also the elaborate plays of Margot Tenenbaum in *The Royal Tenenbaums*). The most striking of these sets is Imdad Khan's (played by Ben Kingsley)

#E8AA36
R232 G170 B54

#D3603C
R211 G96 B60

#CA3C25
R202 G60 B37

#949763
R148 G151 B99

flashback to the Indian jungle, where he recalls meeting the great yogi who taught him clairvoyance. A beautifully painted floral backdrop frames the meeting, and to give the illusion that the yogi is levitating, an obviously camouflaged wooden block is seen in the frame. There is something distinctly handmade about the sequence, as though we are watching a lovingly crafted, but low-budget stage show; seeing set transitions is a feature for Anderson, not a bug. (The effect continues across the Dahl's shorts, as though we are watching the stories come to life directly from Dahl's mind.)

After reading the account of Imdad Khan, Henry becomes obsessed with mastering clairvoyance and sequesters himself away inside his home for months, focusing on the light of a flickering candle. Although the apartment does not change—we see various orderly and extravagant rooms—Henry's appearance becomes comically unkempt for a moment, with a scraggly beard and long hair, until he finally emerges having mastered the skill. He enters a casino to try it out [OPPOSITE]—the building resembles Henry's home, with its opulent fittings and apparent formal dress code, implying this is very much the world he belongs to and providing a stark contrast to the jungles of Imdad's portion of the story (though Kingsley appears again as a casino dealer). But as he discovers his plan has worked, Henry is surprised to realize that his interest in accumulating money has dissipated somewhat.

#CED390
R206 G211 B144

#06D060
R6 G208 B96

#C23204
R194 G50 B4

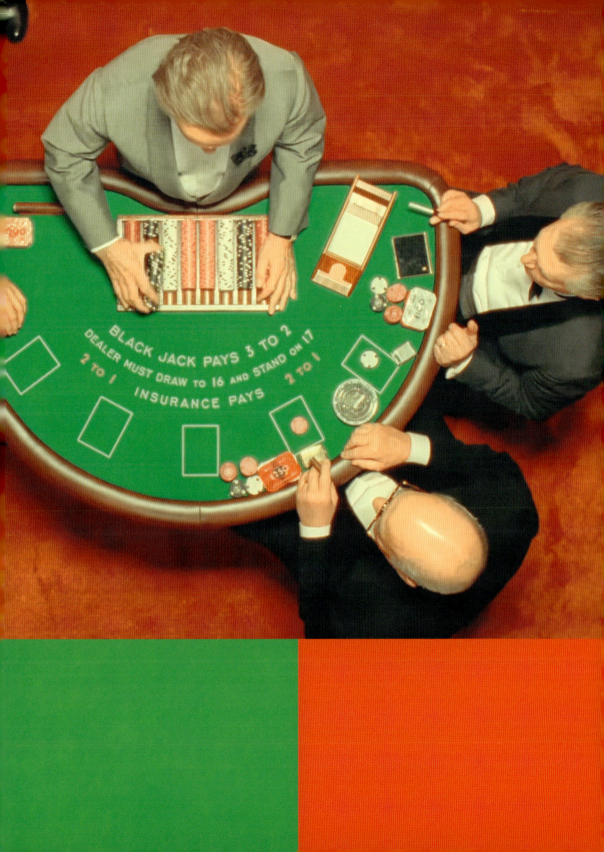

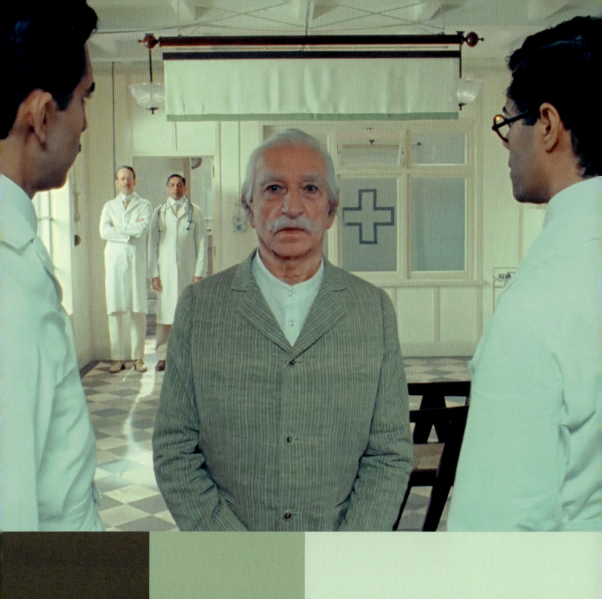

#404036
R64 G54 B54

#94B282
R148 G178 B130

#D2EBB6
R210 G235 B182

He decides he will give his fortune away. He stands on the roof of his London flat wearing his smart red pyjamas, which had previously been a symbol of his well-to-do status. But now, against the gray skyline, they feel like an eccentric affectation, particularly when he begins throwing wads of banknotes down to passers-by in the street, causing chaos. Notably, Henry's attire differs greatly from that of the unassuming carnival performer Imdad Khan, who dresses quite simply [TOP]. Yet, the hospital set used in the Khan portion of the story is reused in a scene with Henry, further tying their narratives together [BOTTOM]. Here, Henry's red pyjamas stand out against the light colors of the hospital corridors, providing a striking visual contrast.

At the close of the film, Dahl's home is revealed again, and he explains that he was entrusted with Henry Sugar's story by that same accountant, on the proviso that he does not use Sugar's real name. The bright warmth of *The Wonderful Story of Henry Sugar* reflects its optimistic message about discovering one's true purpose and that contentment comes from within (suffice to say, the story differs quite dramatically from the other three in the collection). Although visually distinct from his version of *Fantastic Mr. Fox,* Anderson's film retains the sense of whimsy and creativity that is so present across Dahl's work; it also ties together *Henry Sugar* with the three shorter Dahl films through the application of a similar color palette [PAGES 156–57].

#8AB390
R138 G179 B144

#D9423C
R217 G66 B60

THE THING WITH FEATHERS

THE SWAN
2023

The Swan has the unique distinction of being Wes Anderson's most unsettling film to date—no mean feat considering it is only 17 minutes long. Despite tackling heavy topics such as suicide, parental death, and drug addiction within his body of work, there is something disarmingly raw and simple about *The Swan*, which depicts a horrific act of bullying inflicted on the narrator, Peter Watkins (Rupert Friend), who recalls the incident from his childhood.

Set in the English countryside, against a stark white backdrop [TOP], Anderson uses hidden doors in hay bales and undergrowth to bring a theatrical element to *The Swan*, a feature of all the Roald Dahl shorts. It is, on the surface, quite a simple film, in which a young boy (and keen birdwatcher) is relentlessly bullied by two older boys armed with a rifle. After shooting some birds, they decide to torment Peter, first by tying him to the train tracks [BOTTOM] and allowing a train to pass over him. The adult Peter Watkins' outfit blends into the gray foreground, contrasting with the golden hay bales behind, and emphasizing the helplessness he must have felt in this moment. When Peter survives, they take him to a nearby lake, and carry out an even more devastating act of cruelty, killing and butchering a swan and tying its mutilated wings to Peter's arms.

Given that this is a Wes Anderson film, *The Swan* is not particularly graphic, but this makes the small touches of violence all the more meaningful. A collection of dead birds displayed proudly on a string is unnerving, while the red blood spattered on the wings that Peter is forced to wear contrasts boldly with the white of the feathers [PAGES 160–61]. It is an indelible indicator of the horror of the bullying incident, and the callousness of Peter's tormentors. The sparse set and rigid, formal way in which the characters move create an eerie, serious tone, compounded by the misery that Peter endures.

If there is a small reprieve, it is knowing that Peter survived to recall the incident in his early thirties, but this does not negate how chilling *The Swan* is, both in its use of dazzling white and the utility of its production. Gone is Anderson's signature whimsy, stripped back to something sadder and more shocking. It is a haunting display that evokes Richie's suicide attempt from *The Royal Tenenbaums* in somberness, but also captures how blunt and bleak the writing of Roald Dahl could be. It is of little surprise that Anderson should find kinship with him as an artist. Both are associated with boundless imagination and a distinct, unique tweeness, but devotees know the tragic depths that lurk beneath the surface.

 #485A4E R72 G90 B98

 #CAA869 R202 G168 B105

 #E4F0D8 R228 G240 B216

 #676453 R103 G100 B83

 #CAA869 R202 G168 B105

 #0F697D R15 G105 B125

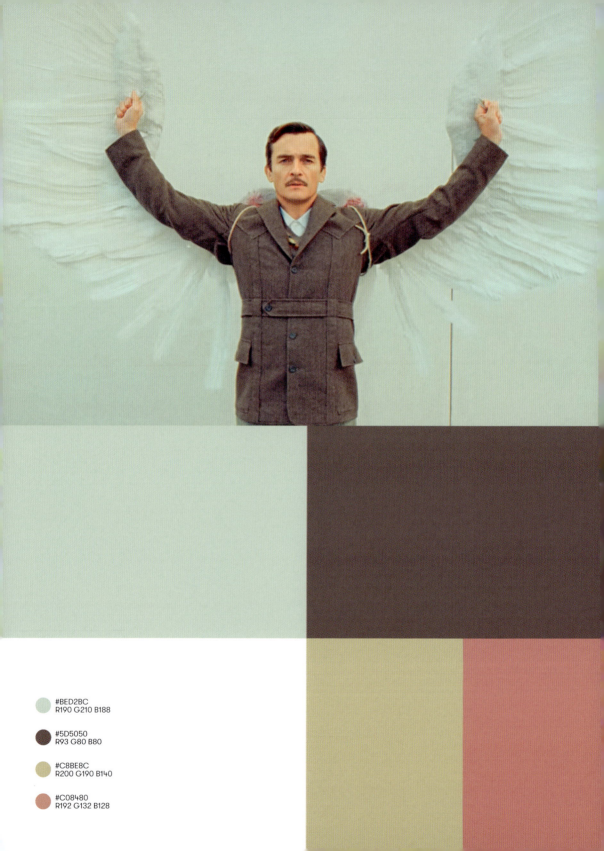

TOOTH AND CLAW

THE RAT CATCHER 2023

For this adaptation of a short story from Dahl's 1953 collection *Someone Like You*, Wes Anderson recruited Ralph Fiennes to play the titular rat catcher. Spotted prosthetic teeth and a gray wig give him the distinctly ratty appearance of the pest control expert who arrives to take care of a vermin problem. As with the other Dahl shorts, *The Rat Catcher* is set in an unspecified (but likely contemporary-to-the-author) British past, and designed as though it were a play, complete with matte paintings. The most splendid of these is the yellow skyline that appears behind Rat Man [TOP], a foreboding sunset that blackens at the top, foreshadowing the strange nightmare the Editor (Richard Ayoade), who narrates the story, is about to bear witness to.

The sinister look of Fiennes—stained brown jacket, patched brown pants, yellowing fingernails, and unkempt hair—is compounded by brown contact lenses, which give his eyes a beady edge [BOTTOM]. Dahl's story strongly implies that the rat catcher may be part rat himself, and that is taken to heart here. There is an air of creeping dread that ramps up when the rat catcher is unsuccessful in poisoning the creatures that live in the haystack.

After a violent display involving a rat and a ferret (mercifully described, but not shown), a rat puppet appears on "stag" in a box labeled "Props Department"—also seen in *The Wonderful Story of Henry Sugar*—to add a slight moment of charming relief. The puppet resembles the sinister Rat, voiced by Willem Dafoe in *Fantastic Mr. Fox*, albeit without the stylish threads [PAGE 164], and will meet a similarly unpleasant end. As he stands in front of the three men, he looks awfully similar to his human antagonist, with matted brown-gray fur. Here Anderson changes technique slightly. Rupert Friend (who plays Claude the mechanic in the short) pops in some false teeth to play the rat for a moment, as he faces off against Rat Man in a bizarre display, after the latter bets a shilling he can kill the rat without touching it.

The scene darkens, with the light source shrinking only to illuminate the Editor and the faces of Friend and Fiennes as they clash. In a simply choreographed fight scene, the rat catcher performs a strange ritual and then bites the rat just as the Editor looks away. The red blood stains his teeth, giving him a vampiric appearance. He explains to the horrified Editor and Claude that rat's blood is used to make liquorice, before scampering away silently (rat-like) into the afternoon, leaving his audience—both the Editor and Claude, and us—thoroughly uncomfortable [PAGE 165].

It's a disquieting little story, but Roald Dahl was known for his great love of the macabre. In Wes Anderson's hands, even the grotesque becomes a little bit stylish.

#D8A200
R216 G162 B0

#9D774C
R1157 G119 B76

#AFC6AB
R175 G198 B171

#646258
R100 G98 B88

#787D73
R120 G125 B115

#2E231A
R46 G35 B36

#A48428
R96 G108 B88

#C29C2C
R194 G156 B44

#FBD2A6
R251 G210 B166

SNAKE BITES

POISON
2023

Set in India during the British Raj, *Poison* was first published in American *Collier*'s magazine in 1950 but would go on to have quite a long life, appearing again in the short-story collection *Someone Like You*. It was later adapted twice for television—first by Alfred Hitchcock in 1958 (he adapted several of Dahl's shorts) and again in 1980 for *Roald Dahl's Tales of the Unexpected*. The latter was introduced by the author himself, who claimed it was inspired by an incident that occurred when he was twenty, working in Tanzania, and saw a gardener die from a snake bite.

Needless to say, Anderson had his work cut out creating his own distinct version, but it helps that both previous entities were quite different from the source material. Wes Anderson's *Poison* is more faithful to the original and is notable as a work that directly engages with racism (something that Anderson has been criticized for neglecting to address in the past, particularly regarding *The Darjeeling Limited* and *Isle of Dogs*, and the lack of diversity among their casts).

The plot is deceptively simple: Timber Woods (Dev Patel) returns to the bungalow he shares with his housemate Harry Pope (Benedict Cumberbatch), only to find Harry in a curious predicament. Namely, he is lying completely still in bed, having seen a small black-and-white snake (a krait) slither under the sheet. Terrified he is about to be bitten, he cannot move. Woods immediately calls Dr Ganderbai (Ben Kingsley), who arrives and performs an expert snake extraction . . . only for it to be revealed there was never any snake at all. Harry, humiliated and furious, directs a racist tirade at the Indian doctor, much to Timber's horror.

As in the three other Dahl shorts he directed, Anderson maintains a stage set-up and a neutral-heavy color palette, here relying on swampy greens, creams, and browns [OPPOSITE], with the occasional pop of color (the book Harry is reading in bed, *The Golden Lotus*, stands out for its green-and-yellow cover [PAGES 168–69]). Visually, the short ties in with the other films in the series, which share a visual language and rotating cast (Dev Patel, Benedict Cumberbatch, and Ben Kingsley return from *The Wonderful Story of Henry Sugar*).

The relative simplicity of *Poison* does not detract from the tension of the story or the shocking moment when Harry unleashes a vile tirade against Dr Ganderbai, who does not respond. But as the doctor leaves, we see a sign reading "British Jute," a reminder of the specter of colonialism and the insidious way in which dominant cultures can turn against minorities when they no longer see them as useful.

#00548C
R0 G84 B140

#74787E
R116 G120 B126

#5C3414
R92 G52 B20

#645E36
R100 G94 B54

#A78761
R167 G135 B97

#8B8B72
R139 G139 B114

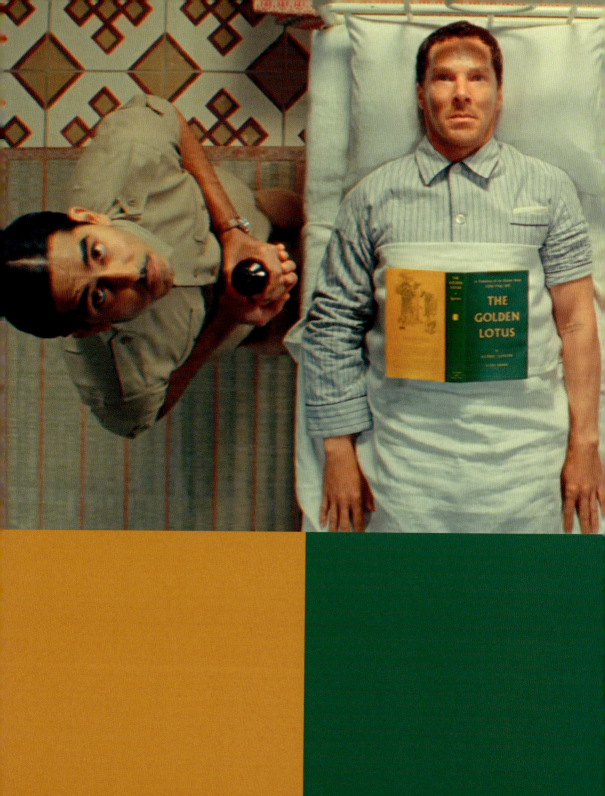

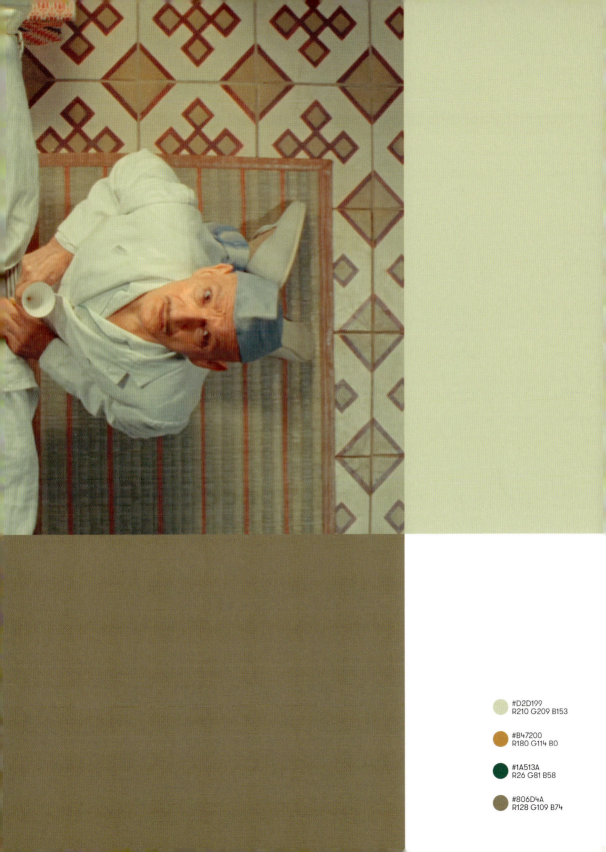

INDEX

Academy Awards 11–12, 48
adverts 90–3
Ahluwalia, Waris 90
"Aline" music video 132–5
Allen, Woody 26
Altman, Robert, *M*A*S*H* 112
American Express, 'My Life, My Card' 90
amusement, color as 68
Anderson, Eric 9
Anderson, Mel 9
Anderson, Melver 9
Anderson, Texas 9
animals 44–7
animation
    Fantastic Mr. Fox 11, 82–9
    Isle of Dogs 116–23
    The Life Aquatic with Steve Zissou 58, 82
Anno, Hideaki 114
Argento, Dario 21
Aristotle 21
art, fine 114
Asteroid City 12–13, 62, 140–9, 150
    Jake Ryan 91
    Jarvis Cocker 114
    Rupert Friend 92
    use of black and white in 68, 128, 140, 144
    use of yellow in 138
AT&T 90
Auerbach, Frank 114
Ayoade, Richard 162
Aznarez, Javi 132

Bacon, Francis 114
Balaban, Bob 94
Baldwin, Alec 112
Bande à part 112
Baudraud, Edith 114
Baumbach, Noal 11
Beach Boys 85
the Beatles 136
The Big Shave 112
black, use of
    The Darjeeling Limited 74
    The Grand Budapest Hotel 68, 109–10

black and white, use of 19
    Asteroid City 68, 128, 140, 144
    Bottle Rocket 26, 68
    The French Dispatch 68, 124, 128, 138
    The Grand Budapest Hotel 68
    The Royal Tenenbaums 45
Blanchett, Cate 62–5
The Bling Ring 21
blue, use of 19–20, 21
    Bottle Rocket 66
    The Darjeeling Limited 74
    The French Dispatch 128
    Hotel Chevalier 78
    The Life Aquatic with Steve Zissou 58, 62, 67
    Moonrise Kingdom 67, 99
    The Royal Tenenbaums 48, 52, 67
    Rushmore 44, 66
bokeh 109
Bottle Rocket 11, 26–33, 34, 112, 136
    short film version 10, 13, 26, 68
    use of black and white in 26, 68
    use of red in 30, 66
Bramesco, Charles 19
Breathless 30
Bresson, Robert 112
Britten, Benjamin, *Noye's Fludde* 94, 99
Brody, Adrien
    Asteroid City 144
    The Darjeeling Limited 70–7
    The Grand Budapest Hotel 109–11
    H&M advert 92
Brooks, James L. 10, 26
Brooks, Richard 128
brown, use of
    Fantastic Mr. Fox 46, 82
    The Royal Tenenbaums 52
Bruegel, Pieter the Elder 114
bunraku 120
burgundy, use of 78

Cannes Film Festival 12
Capote, Truman 128

Carson, L. M. Kit 11
Cassavetes, John,
    Husbands 70
Castello Cavalcanti (Prada) 92
Cera, Michael 13
Chaffin, Donald 85
Chalamet, Timothée 12, 132
Chang, Justin 120
Close Encounters of the Third Kind 144
Cocker, Jarvis 114
    "Aline" 132–5
Collider 94
Collier's 166
color
    as a form of communication 66–9
    color in film 18–23
'Come Together: A Fashion Picture in Motion' (H&M) 92
communication, imperfect 66
Coppola, Eleanor 94
Coppola, Roman 11
    The Darjeeling Limited 70
    Isle of Dogs 116
    Moonrise Kingdom 12, 94
    The Phoenician Scheme 13
    Prada Candy L'eau 92
    Stella Artois 91
Coppola, Sofia 132
    The Bling Ring 21
    Marie Antoinette 70
Cousteau, Jacques 58, 62
Cousteau, Philippe 62
Cox, Brian 34
Cranston, Bryan 120
Criterion Collection 21
Cumberbatch, Benedict
    Poison 166
    The Wonderful Story of Henry Sugar 150–5

Dafoe, Willem
    Fantastic Mr. Fox 162
    The Grand Budapest Hotel 109–11
Dahl, Roald 9, 92, 138, 150

Fantastic Mr. Fox 11, 46, 82, 85, 116, 136
  Poison 46, 150, 155, 166–9
  The Rat Catcher 150, 155, 162–5
  Someone Like You 162, 166
  The Swan 150, 155, 158–61
  The Wonderful Story of Henry Sugar 12, 150–7
danger, sense of 68
the *Darjeeling Limited* 67, 70–7, 114
  animals in 46
  Hotel Chevalier 78, 137
  Jason Schwartzman 11, 70
  racism 166
dark shades 20
Day For Night 62
Dazed 114
de Kooning, Willem 114
Dean, James 144
Demy, Jacques 112, 114
Diabolique 128
dialogue 66

Enderle, Curt 116

Fantastic Mr Fox (book) 9, 82
Fantastic Mr. Fox (film) 11, 13, 67, 68, 82–9, 91, 116, 144, 155
  Anderson's fascination with animals 44, 46
  Jarvis Cocker 114
  use of yellow in 46, 82, 86, 136, 137
  Willem Dafoe 162
Fiennes, Ralph
  The Grand Budapest Hotel 12, 104–11
  The Rat Catcher 162–5
  The Wonderful Story of Henry Sugar 150–5
Fincher, David 34, 132
fine art 114
The Fire Within 48, 112
Focus Features 144
The 400 Blows 94, 114
The French Dispatch 13, 62, 92, 112, 124–31, 144
  New Yorker 12, 114, 124, 132

Robert Yeoman 124, 140
  use of black and white in 68, 124, 128, 138
  use of yellow in 124, 128, 137–8
French New Wave 112, 128
Friend, Rupert
  Asteroid City 92
  Montblanc advert 92
  The Rat Catcher 162
  The Swan 158
Fujii, Moeko 120

Gaiman, Neil 82
Gilman, Jared, *Moonrise Kingdom* 94–100
Glover, Danny 11
Godard, Jean-Luc 30
  Bande à part 112
  Diabolique 128
  Vivre sa vie 128
golden colors, use of
  Fantastic Mr. Fox 136
  Moonrise Kingdom 136
  The Royal Tenenbaums 52
Golden Globe 10, 11
Goodall, Jane 62
The Graduate 112
The Grand Budapest Hotel 12, 62, 66, 67, 92, 104–11, 114
  use of black in 68, 109–10
  use of pink in 104, 109
gray, use of
  The Darjeeling Limited 74
  The Grand Budapest Hotel 110
green, use of 20, 22
  Asteroid City 68
  The Darjeeling Limited 74
  Rushmore 44
Gustafson, Mark, *Fantastic Mr. Fox* 82

H&M, "Come Together: A Fashion Picture in Motion" 92
Hackman, Gene 11, 48–57
Harrod, Paul 116
Hartley, L.P., *The Go-Between* 110
Hayward, Kara, *Moonrise Kingdom* 94–100
Heat 114

Henson, Jim 46
Hitchcock, Alfred 9, 166
Hokusai, Katsushika 114, 116
Holbein, Hans the Younger 114
Hotel Chevalier 78–81, 137
Husbands 70
Huston, Angelica
  The French Dispatch 124
  The Royal Tenenbaums 11, 48
Hyundai
  "Modern Life" 91
  "Talk To My Car" 91

Ikea 91
  "Unböring" campaign 90
In Cold Blood 128
In The Mood For Love 21
inclusion, sense of 67–8
Isle of Dogs 12, 68, 82, 116–23, 137, 144, 166
  animals in 44, 46
  influence of Katsushika Hokusai 114, 116
Italian Renaissance 114

Jarmusch, Jim 26
Johansson, Scarlett 140
Jonze, Spike 34, 132
Jules et Jim 92, 114
khaki, use of 67, 99

Kilmer, Val 114
Kingsley, Ben
  Poison 166
  The Wonderful Story of Henry Sugar 150, 152–5
the Kinks 114
Kopp, Sandro 114
Kurosawa, Akira 116

"Le Apartomatic" (Stella Artois) 91
Lee, Bruce 136
Les Enfants terrible 136
Les Vacances de Monsieur Hulot 90
The Life Aquatic with Steve Zissou 11, 44, 46, 58–65, 68, 70, 94, 114, 144

animation 58, 82
　　use of blue in 58, 62, 67
　　use of red in 58, 67
　　use of yellow in 62, 136, 137
Looney Tunes 140
Los Angeles Times 120
Lowry, Nelson 82

M*A*S*H 112
McDormand, Frances 132
"Made of Imagination" (Sony) 91
magical realism 140
The Magnificent Ambersons 48, 112
Malle, Louis, The Fire Within 48, 112
Malouf, Juman 12
Mann, Michael, Heat 114
Méliès, Georges 19
Melville, Jean-Pierre 136
metallic colors, use of 68, 120
mid-century modern design 91
Miyazaki, Hayao 116
"Modern Life" (Hyundai) 91
Monroe, Marilyn 144
Montblanc 92
Moonrise Kingdom 12, 46, 94–103, 114
　　use of blue in 67, 99
　　use of pink in 99, 100
　　use of yellow in 100, 136–7
Murray, Bill
　　The Life Aquatic with Steve Zissou 58–65
　　The Royal Tenenbaums 11
　　Rushmore 10, 34, 37, 40, 44
Musgrave, Robert 26
music 114
　　"Aline" video 132–5
"My Life, My Card" (American Express) 90

neon 19, 128
Netflix 150
The New Yorker 12, 91, 114, 120, 124, 132
Nichols, Mike 112
Nomura, Kunichi, Isle of Dogs 116
Norton, Edward 140

On with the Show! 19
Ophüls, Max 114
orange, use of
　　"Aline" 132
　　The Darjeeling Limited 74
　　Fantastic Mr. Fox 46, 82, 86
　　The French Dispatch 128
orphans 94
Oscar nominations 11–12, 48
Otomo, Katsuhiro 116
Ozu, Yasujirō 114

Paltrow, Gwyneth 11, 48–57
pastels 20, 22, 34, 67, 68, 104
Patel, Dev 166
Peissel, Octavia 132
Pellegrino, Rich 114
The Phoenician Scheme 13
Picasso, Pablo 114
pink, use of 20
　　The French Dispatch 128
　　The Grand Budapest Hotel 104, 109
　　Moonrise Kingdom 99, 100
Pitt, Brad, SoftBank advert 90, 112
Poison 46, 150, 155, 166–9
Portman, Natalie, Hotel Chevalier 78–81
Powell, Michael 112
Prada
　　Castello Cavalcanti 92
　　Prada Candy L'eau 92
Pressburger, Emeric 112
Pulp 114
purple, use of 67, 104

The Rat Catcher 138, 150, 155, 162–5
ravens 99
Ray, Satyajit 74, 114
realism 140
red, use of 19, 21
　　Bottle Rocket 30, 66
　　Fantastic Mr. Fox 46, 82, 86
　　The French Dispatch 128
　　The Grand Budapest Hotel 104
　　The Life Aquatic with Steve Zissou 58, 67

The Royal Tenenbaums 48, 52, 67
Rushmore 37, 40, 66
The Wonderful Story of Henry Sugar 150, 155
The Red Shoes 112
Renoir, Jean 70, 74
The River 70
Roald Dahl's Tales of the Unexpected 166
Rolling Stones 85, 112, 114
Roth, Joe 10
Rothko, Mark 114
The Royal Tenenbaums 10–11, 44–5, 48–57, 62, 66, 90, 112, 150, 158
　　use of blue in 48, 52, 67
　　use of red in 48, 52, 67
　　use of white in 48, 52, 67
　　use of yellow in 52, 67, 136, 138
Rushmore 9, 10, 34–43, 44, 48, 66, 67, 112
Ryan, Jake 91, 140

Sallinger, J.D., Franny & Zooey 48
Schiele, Egon 114
Schwartzman, Jason 10, 34–43, 44
　　American Express advert 90
　　Asteroid City 13, 140
　　Castello Cavalcanti 92
　　The Darjeeling Limited 11, 70
　　Hotel Chevalier 78–81
　　Isle of Dogs 116
　　Montblanc advert 92
Scorsese, Martin 70, 112
Seitz, Matt Zoller, The Wes Anderson Collection 58
self-expression, color as 66–9
Selick, Henry 44, 58, 82
sepia 19
Seydoux, Léa
　　The French Dispatch 92
　　The Grand Budapest Hotel 92
　　Prada Candy L'eau 92
shadow puppetry 120
silver, use of 68, 120
Small Change 94

Smith, Elliott 52
Smith, Sian 114
Snow White and the Seven Dwarves 19
Soderbergh, Steven 34
SoftBank 90–1, 112
Sony, "Made of Imagination" advert 91
Star Trek 58
Star Wars 9, 19–20
Stella Artois, "Le Apartomatic" 91
Stern, Phil 144
Stiller, Ben 11, 48–57
Stockhause, Adam 116
Sundance Film Festival 10, 26
The Swan 150, 155, 158–61
Swinton, Tilda, *The Grand Budapest Hotel* 114

"Talk To My Car" (Hyundai) 91
Tarantino, Quentin 12, 26, 112
Tati, Jacques 112, 128
    Les Vacances de Monsieur Hulot 90
Taylor, Michael 114
Technicolor 20
Threapleton, Mia 13
timeline 16–17
Tokyo Story 114
Toro, Benicio del 13
Touchstone Pictures 10
A Trip to the Moon 19
Truffaut, François 112
    The 400 Blows 94, 114
    Day For Night 62, 90
    Jules et Jim 92
    Small Change 94

The Umbrellas of Cherbourg 112
"Unboring" campaign (Ikea) 90

Vallotton, Félix 114
Varda, Agnès 112
Vivre sa vie 128

Warner Bros 19
Weir, Peter, *Witness* 114

Welles, Orson, *The Magnificent Ambersons* 48, 112
white, use of 20
    The Darjeeling Limited 74
    The Royal Tenenbaums 48, 52, 67
    see also black and white
Wilde, Olivia 44
Williams, Olivia 34–43
Wilson, Andrew 9, 136
Wilson, Luke 9
    Bottle Rocket 26–33
    The Royal Tenenbaums 11, 48–57
Wilson, Owen 9–10
    Bottle Rocket 26–33, 112
    The Darjeeling Limited 70–7
    The Grand Budapest Hotel 110
    The Royal Tenenbaums 11, 48–57
The Wizard of Oz 20
The Wonderful Story of Henry Sugar 12, 138, 150–7, 162
Wong Kar-Wai 21
Wright, Jeffrey 12, 128

yellow, use of 21, 34, 136–9
    "Aline" 132
    Asteroid City 138
    Bottle Rocket 30, 66, 136
    Castello Cavalcanti 92
    The Darjeeling Limited 137
    Fantastic Mr. Fox 46, 82, 86, 136, 137
    The French Dispatch 124, 128, 137–8
    Hotel Chevalier 78, 137
    Isle of Dogs 137
    The Life Aquatic with Steve Zissou 62, 136, 137
    Moonrise Kingdom 100, 136–7
    The Rat Catcher 138
    The Royal Tenenbaums 52, 67, 136, 138
    Rushmore 37
    SoftBank advert 90
    The Wonderful Story of Henry Sugar 150

Yeoman, Robert
    Asteroid City 144
    Bottle Rocket 26
    The French Dispatch 124, 140
    Rushmore 34
The Young Girls of Rochefort 112

ACKNOWLEDGMENTS

It has been an honor and a joy to take such a deep dive into the work of a filmmaker whose work means the world to me. One of my very first professional writing commissions was on the films of Wes Anderson; I never would have imagined that less than a decade later, I would be writing a book about him. I am extremely grateful to Alice Graham at Quarto, who thought of me for the project, and provided me with so much encouragement and support throughout the process. I must also thank the rest of the team at Quarto for their sound guidance and hard work: Laura Bulbeck, Anna Southgate, Isabel Eeles, Trystan Thompson.

Of course, thanks to Wes Anderson for all the movies. You'll never read this, but you really did get me through some of the worst years of my life.

I would also like to extend my gratitude to my dear friend Charles Bramesco, whose book *Colors of Film* paved the way for this title, and whose work provided a sturdy foundation. You have been an inspiration throughout my career, as well as a supportive colleague and a wonderful friend. Along these lines, I would like to thank fellow Wes Anderson scholars and enthusiasts, David Jenkins, Adam Woodward, and Sophie Monks Kaufman, who are similarly encouraging and inspiring. I consider myself very fortunate to have talented colleagues who are also tip-top human beings.

Special shout-out to my darlings Rafa Sales Ross, Leila Latif, and Marshall Schaffer, who gamely endured many of my rants while I was in the depths of writing. Big love to the TIFF group chat too, who also put up with some good-natured moaning over the past year.

Endless love to my mum, my siblings (Jonathon and Eleanor), and to my uncles (Rod and Simon), whose love of the arts was a huge influence on me as a child. And finally, thanks to my very own Margot Tenenbaum, a tiny cat, who did nothing but look cute and provide moral support.

This book is dedicated to Audrey Strong, whom I think of every single day.

ABOUT THE AUTHOR

Hannah Strong is an author, editor, and critic from Sheffield, United Kingdom. The first Wes Anderson film she saw was *The Royal Tenenbaums*, sparking a lifelong fascination with his work. She lives in London, with her cat Margot, and can frequently be found haunting cinemas all around the world. Her first book, *Sofia Coppola: Forever Young* was published in 2022. She serves as the Digital Editor at *Little White Lies* magazine, and has appeared in print, online, on radio, and on television in her capacity as an arts journalist. *Colors of Wes Anderson* is her second book.

Quarto

First published in 2025 by Frances Lincoln,
an imprint of The Quarto Group.
One Triptych Place, London,
SE1 9SH, United Kingdom
T (0)20 7700 9000
www.Quarto.com

EEA Representation, WTS Tax d.o.o.,
Žanova ulica 3, 4000 Kranj, Slovenia
www.wts-tax.si

Text Copyright © 2025 Hannah Strong
Design Copyright © 2025 Quarto Publishing plc
Images: Film stills copyright © the relevant film production and distribution companies. Front cover: TCD/Prod DB © Indian Paintbrush - American Empirical - Scott Rudin Productions/Alamy; 14–15: © Focus Features/Entertainment Pictures/ZUMAPRESS.com/Alamy; 113 bottom: TCD/Prod.DB © Martin Scorsese – New York Uni/Alamy; 175: © Ella Kemp.

Hannah Strong has asserted her moral right to be identified as the Author of this Work in accordance with the Copyright Designs and Patents Act 1988.

All rights reserved. No part of this book may be reproduced or utilized in any form or by any means, electronic or mechanical, including photocopying, recording or by any information storage and retrieval system, without permission in writing from Frances Lincoln.

Every effort has been made to trace the copyright holders of material quoted in this book. If application is made in writing to the publisher, any omissions will be included in future editions.

A catalogue record for this book is available from the British Library.

ISBN 978-1-83600-426-4
Ebook ISBN 978-1-83600-428-8

10 9 8 7 6 5 4 3 2 1

Design by Intercity

Publisher Philip Cooper
Senior Commissioning Editor Alice Graham
Senior Editor Laura Bulbeck
Senior Designer Isabel Eeles
Senior Production Manager Alex Merrett

Printed in Guangdong, China TT062025